TO the KID IN the PEW

60 CHAPEL TALKS— SERIES B

ELDON WEISHEIT

Publishing House
St. Louis   London

Concordia Publishing House, St. Louis, Missouri
Concordia Publishing House Ltd., London, E. C. 1
Copyright © 1975 Concordia Publishing House
MANUFACTURED IN THE UNITED STATES OF AMERICA

Library of Congress Cataloging in Publication Data (Revised)

Weisheit, Eldon.
    To the kid in the pew.

    1. Children's sermons.
BV4315.W375   252'.53   74-4548
ISBN 0-570-03238-5

Preface

Please do not regard these children's sermons as loaves of bakery bread all wrapped and on the shelf ready for you to serve. The book is not intended to be held in one hand as you read from it while you display an object in your other hand. (Used that way, the sermons will sound as though they came from the back shelf of the day-old store: stale.)

Rather use these sermons as a mix. The book contains messages from the Bible and suggestions on how to illustrate the messages. You must always add your own faith and your own knowledge of the people to whom you are speaking. Bake the message in the warmth of your own love for Christ and His people. Then you will have a fresh loaf ready to be served. And your worship will include that sweet smelling savor often mentioned in Scripture.

Doing your own baking means you will have some work to do. Start that work with a study of the text. Object lessons, and other illustrations, become superficial when the object is chosen first and a text is found to support it. Each message in this book started with the text. Only when the Scripture said something to me, could I look for a way to pass the message on to others. You also will have to listen to God's Word before you can find a message from it to share with others.

May the Holy Spirit bless your efforts to communicate the joyful message of Christ the Savior.

ELDON WEISHEIT

Scripture Index

The homilies in this book are based on portions of the Epistles selected by the Inter-Lutheran Commission on Worship, Year B.

To my son
Dirk,
whose questions contributed to the content of this book
on his 17th birthday.

Contents

A Message That Will Last

The Word

The message about Christ has become so firmly fixed in you, that you have not failed to receive a single blessing, as you wait for our Lord Jesus Christ to be revealed. 1 Corinthians 1:6-7 (From the Epistle for the First Sunday in Advent)

The World

A child's jacket, a small piece of paper and several pins, a marker pencil, needle and thread, and a piece of cloth.

Children sometimes have a problem about losing things. This is a nice jacket, for example. But if you took it to school, you could easily lose it. You might leave it in a classroom or forget it on the playground. Or someone might take it from you.

God has a problem something like that—only His problem is more serious. He lost many people—people whom He loved. He lost them not because He misplaced them or forgot where they were but because they ran away from Him. It would be a problem if you lost your jacket, but a jacket can be replaced. God loves each person so none can be replaced.

But both you and God have ways to avoid losing things. First think about you and the jacket. One way to keep from losing the jacket would be to fasten your name to it. If I write my name on this piece of paper and pin it to the jacket, everyone will know it is mine. But the paper could easily be taken off if someone wanted to steal the jacket. Or it could accidentally tear off. Or think what would happen when the jacket was washed.

A better way would be to write your name on this piece of cloth and then sew the cloth to the jacket. (Start sewing —you need not finish.) See—now the name has become a part of the jacket. It won't tear loose, and it can't be pulled off.

God's way to keep from losing us was to send His Son to be our Savior. The story of Advent is about how God promised to save us from being lost, and we will see that promise kept on Christmas. The message of Christ is that God loves us, and He brings us back to God so we are no longer lost.

In our Bible reading St. Paul tells us that the message of Christ has been firmly fixed on us so we have not failed to receive a single blessing. When Christ came to earth, He didn't just drop by for a short visit. Then His message would have been like the name on the piece of paper. His message would not have lasted.

But the message of Christ became "firmly fixed" in us —like the cloth name tag sewn to the garment. All the things that Christ did on earth—including His death for us—firmly fixed on Him in our lives. Because He rose again, He can remain a part of the world forever.

We prepare for Christmas during Advent so the message of Christmas becomes firmly fixed in our own lives. Christmas is not a temporary blessing—like a name on a piece of paper. Christmas tells us that God became a part of our lives and stayed with us. That's worth celebrating.

Slow? Or Patient?

The Word

The Lord is not slow to do what He has promised, as some think. Instead, He is patient with you, because He does not want anyone to be destroyed, but wants all to turn away from their sins. 2 Peter 3:9 (From the Epistle for the Second Sunday in Advent)

The World

Several sheets of Christmas seals.

The Bible reading for today tells us about a job that Christ has promised to do. He has told us that He will come to judge the earth. He made the promise a long time ago. But He still hasn't done it. We have the Advent season to remind ourselves about Christ's promise to come again to be our judge. Each year we hear again about a promise that still hasn't been kept.

Some say that Christ is slow about doing His work. After all, 2,000 years is a long time to wait for anyone — even God. But the Bible reading says that Christ is not slow. Instead He is patient. Let's think about the difference between being slow and being patient.

Suppose your mother told you she needed your help in mailing Christmas cards. Your job is to tear the sheets of Christmas seals into individual seals so she can put them on the envelopes. There are several ways to do the job.

You might think, "I'm in a hurry, so I'm going to get this job done as fast as I can." So you grab the seals and start tearing. (Rip the seals apart so many individual seals are destroyed.) You might get the job done fast that way, but it wouldn't be done right.

Another way would be to take your time. You might think to yourself, "If I am slow, Mom will get tired and do the job for me." (Slowly remove one seal at a time by tearing each small piece of paper.) That is being slow.

The right way to do the job is to take enough time to do it properly and yet get it done as soon as possible. (Fold each row of seals along the perforation and tear the entire row off, then divide the individual seals.) This way you get the job done right. It is being patient.

Christ is also patient about doing His work as our Judge. The Bible reading says He does not want any of us to be destroyed. He doesn't rush Judgment Day just to get it done. He wants all people to know about His work for us. Christ who is our Judge is the same Christ who worked hard for our salvation. He wants all people to receive the blessings of His death and resurrection for us; so He doesn't rush Judgment Day.

On the other hand, Christ is not slow. He is not wasting time with the hope that we will forget His promise to judge the world. He knows He has to complete His work of salvation for the world by having Judgment Day.

But Christ is patient. He wants to do the job right. He wants us all to first know how He has forgiven our sins so we can be judged without being afraid. He carefully shares the message of His love with each of us.

Because Christ is patient we are preparing for another Christmas. Even though we already know about His blessings, He is patient so we can grow in faith and share the faith with others. His patience is another great blessing we receive at Christmas.

Be Happy Always

The Word

Be happy always, pray at all times, be thankful in all circumstances. This is what God wants of you, in your life in Christ Jesus. 1 Thessalonians 5:16-18 (From the Epistle for the Third Sunday in Advent)

The World

A package wrapped as though it arrived in the mail. It is stamped "Fragile" and "Insured" and shows signs of having been smashed. Inside is a broken toy or other gift — use what you have that has already been broken.

Christmas is a happy time of the year because so many good things happen. We have vacations, get gifts, go to parties, see relatives. We almost feel that we don't need the words in our Bible reading today that tell us to be happy always, pray at all times, and to be thankful in all circumstances. It is easy to be happy when everything is going great.

However, even at Christmas time we need to be told to be happy. It is easy to be sad during the Christmas season. Vacation may be dull. You might not get the present you wanted. Even parties and friends can be a disappointment. The Bible reading offers us a special kind of happiness — we can be happy always, even when things are going wrong.

Let's look at it this way. This package comes in the mail for you. A package this time of the year means a gift. So you are happy. You eagerly open up the wrappings and — all the happiness is gone. You have a gift — but it is broken.

You can't enjoy it. Instead of being happy about the gift you are disappointed — and more unhappy than if you had never received the gift.

But wait a minute. Look, the package is insured. The gift is not lost. It will be replaced. There may be a delay — but you will get the gift. So you can be happy even in the circumstances of having a broken gift because you know you will receive the gift again soon.

Christ did something like this for us when He came to earth to be born the Baby of Bethlehem. He came to give us health, forgiveness, love, happiness, and even eternal life with Him. These are the gifts we are going to have. But sometimes the gifts arrive smashed. We aren't always in good health. We are sometimes disappointed. We sometimes feel guilt. We will even die. The gifts that God wants us to have are not always in good condition.

Yet our Bible reading can tell us to be happy always and to be thankful in all circumstances. We can be happy always because the gifts from Christ can never be taken from us. They are insured. The gifts are guaranteed for us because Christ has earned them for us on the cross as He took our punishment and because He rose again from His grave to show us how we also can have His blessings even after we die.

We don't have to pretend we are happy. We can admit we have failures and hurts. Our real happiness is that we know our life is a gift from God. Even when the gift is messed up, we know that God loves us and through Christ straightens us out. Our life is in God's hands. It is insured. We will have the gift forever.

Who Gets the Glory?

The Word

Let us give glory to God! He is able to make you stand firm in your faith, according to the Good News I preach, the message about Jesus Christ, and according to the revelation of the secret truth which was hidden for long ages in the past. Romans 16:25 (From the Epistle for the Fourth Sunday in Advent)

The World

A Christmas gift, wrapped, that a child has made for his or her parents. A potholder is used here, but the sermon can easily be changed to any other child-made gift.

It is fun to receive gifts. But it is also fun to give gifts — when you have something you want to give away. Pretend this is a Christmas gift for your mother from you. You are eager to give it to her because it is something you made especially for her. (Open the package.) See, it is a potholder. Your mother would appreciate such a gift for two reasons. First, she probably can use the potholder. But more important she would appreciate it because you made the gift for her.

During the Christmas season your mother would show her gifts to friends. Each time she showed the potholder, she would tell everyone you had made it for her. Her friends would also enjoy seeing the gift you had made. They might tell you they admired the colors you chose or the pattern you made. Your mother would have received the gift — but you would have received the attention.

Something like that happens with our Christmas gift

from God. We receive the gift. God sends us His Son to be a part of our lives. Through Christ we receive the Good News mentioned in our Bible reading for today. Because God gave us Christ, we know how much He loves us, and we know that He will always be with us.

But the Bible reading also tells us something else. It says, "Let us give God the glory!" We receive the gift — but God gets the glory. He is the one who planned the gift. He was willing to make the sacrifice for us. When we tell others about the wonderful gift we got from God for Christmas, they all give attention to the One who gave the gift.

In a few days we will hear the Christmas message of the angels who told the shepherds about Jesus' birth. They said that we received the gift of peace on earth and they gave glory to God. Remember their song: "Glory to God in the highest heaven! And peace on earth to men with whom He is pleased!"

Get ready not only to receive the gift that God gives us in Christ but also get ready to give God the glory. He gave us this gift because of His great love for us. We didn't earn it. We can't give Him a gift in exchange. Yet God gives us the greatest gift ever given to anyone. When we show our joy and happiness, we are giving glory to God. When we tell others about the gift we received and who gave it to us, we give glory to God.

Look Who Is Here!

The Word

In the past God spoke to our ancestors many times and in many ways through the prophets, but in these last days He has spoken to us through His Son. . . . [The Son of God] shines with the brightness of God's glory; He is the exact likeness of God's own being. Hebrews 1:1-2a, 3a (From the Epistle for Christmas Day)

The World

Select one child known by most of the others, and ask him or her to be out of view at the beginning of the sermon. Have a large poster saying, "Merry Christmas," signed by the same child. Also have that child's voice saying, "Merry Christmas to all my friends at _____" on a cassette player. (This part may be omitted if impractical.)

Isn't it fun to receive Christmas cards? Here is a greeting from someone whom most of you know. (Show the poster.) Judy remembers all of you and sent this greeting to wish you a merry Christmas. The greeting shows she is thinking about you, and she wants you to enjoy the celebration of the Savior's birth.

Of course, it would be even nicer to hear Judy's voice. And that's possible. Listen! (Play the cassette greeting.) Not only did she think about us, but she recorded her greeting for us.

But there is even a better way to receive Christmas greetings from Judy. That is to see her and have her with us. Come here, Judy. Do you have something to say to your friends here? (Prepare her to say at least "Merry Christmas" or a longer more personal Christmas greeting.)

17

You received the same message three different ways. Each message was from Judy, and each had the same purpose. Yet it is always better to be with a friend than only to receive a card or hear a voice. It is also true that it is better to be with God than only to receive a message from Him through others.

Our Bible reading tells us that in times past—that is in Old Testament times—God spoke through prophets. You've heard the message of Isaiah, Jeremiah, and other prophets. They told us how God loved us and planned to send a Savior. They gave us a happy message from God.

But then the Bible reading says that in those times—that is in New Testament times, God spoke to the world by sending His Son. It says, "The Son of God shines with the brightness of God's glory; He is the exact likeness of God's own being."

Not only did God think about us and send us a message of His love. He also came to be with us. The greeting we have from God today is not just a message sent through others. God Himself came to earth to be born as our brother. He became a part of our lives so He could be our Savior.

Because Christ rose from the dead, He is able to continue to live with us. He is present with us today. He fills our lives with His love and mercy. He shares our sorrows and disappointments. He does not just tell us to have a merry Christmas. He delivers a merry Christmas to us by coming to be with us.

A Gift with All the Extras

The Word

You are the people of God; He loved you and chose you for His own. Therefore, you must put on compassion, kindness, humility, gentleness, and patience. Colossians 3:12 (From the Epistle for the First Sunday After Christmas)

The World

A child's toy that comes with extras. In this sermon a doll with extra dresses and accessories in the same gift kit is used. Other items for children may be substituted.

Remember all of the excitement when you opened Christmas packages a few days ago. You were eager to find out what was in the wrappings. Then after you had opened the package, you probably wanted to use the gift right away. If you opened this box, you would have known what you received — a doll. See what a nice doll it is. If you had wanted a doll, you would probably have taken it from the box to hold it as fast as you could. After you had looked it all over, you would have shown the rest of your family your new doll. Then you would have had time to play with your gift.

Later on, as you looked back over the wrappings and boxes, you would have noticed that there were other things in the box with the doll. See, here is an extra dress, a purse, even a change of shoes for your doll. Of course the doll is the real gift. If someone asks what you received, you will say, "I got a doll." But all the other things are nice gifts that are extras with the doll.

You also received extras with your Christmas gift from God. You know that God gave you His Son to be your Savior. Because God gave you that special Christmas gift, you know that God will be a part of your life always. Our Bible reading for today says it this way, "You are the people of God; He loved you and chose you for His own."

On Christmas Day we were excited about the great gift—as we should have been. But now let's stop to see what we received with the gift. Like the gift of the doll, God's gift has extras. The Bible reading tells us about them when it says, "Therefore, you must put on compassion, kindness, humility, gentleness, and patience."

Because we received Christ we can also have compassion—that means we have feelings for other people; kindness—that's when we show those feelings by helping others; humility—that means we realize that the good we do for others is a gift from God, and He gets the credit; gentleness—that's a way to help make other people comfortable; and patience—that's being willing to keep trying to use all these gifts even after we have failed many times.

These gifts are not separate from the gift of Christ to us. Because Christ gave us His compassion, kindness, humility, gentleness, and patience, we also have received those gifts to give to others. Just like the dress and the accessories went with the doll, these spiritual gifts go with Jesus.

Let's not forget to use all the gifts God has given us. Think now of the times you need those extra gifts. Remember you have Jesus—so you have the gifts that come with Him.

What's in a Name?

The Word

The Good News was promised long ago by God through His prophets, and written in the Holy Scriptures. It is about His Son, our Lord Jesus Christ, as to His humanity, He was born a descendant of David; as to His divine holiness, He was shown with great power to be the Son of God, by being raised from death. Romans 1:2-4 (From the Epistle for the Name of Jesus)

The World

A pencil with an eraser and a piece of paper.

When Mary and Joseph named their baby who had been born in the manger, they called Him Jesus. That was a good Jewish name. It was the name His family and friends called Him. But we have other names for Jesus. Our Bible reading tells us that God's Good News promised by the prophets is seen in His Son, our Lord Jesus Christ. Here we are calling Jesus Lord, which means He is the ruler of our lives, and Christ, which means He is the one God appointed to be our Savior.

In one sense the name of the Savior is unimportant. His parents could have named Him Fred and, because He died and rose again, He would still be our Savior. Yet there is something important about His names—because they help us understand what He did for us. What we call Him shows how we recognize Him and what we need from Him.

This is an illustration: If a friend wanted to write a phone number and asked for a pencil, you would give the friend this (the pencil). (Write a number on the paper.) After the friend had returned the pencil, he might discover that he had written the wrong number. If so, the friend would ask for an eraser. Again you would give him this (the pencil). (Erase and correct the number.) Notice that one time the friend asked for a pencil and another time for an eraser — two different things — yet in each case you gave the friend the same thing. Which is this (the pencil), a pencil or an eraser? Of course, it is both but you use the name that tells what you need.

The same is true of Jesus. We can call Him Jesus, a human name, or we can call Him Lord or Christ which are divine names. The Bible reading says, "The Good News is about His Son, our Lord Jesus Christ: as to His humanity, He was born a descendant of David; as to His divine holiness, He was shown with great power to be the Son of God by being raised from death."

The Lord Jesus Christ is one person, but He is both a human being and God. The pencil is only an illustration about Jesus. It does not show exactly what Jesus is because the eraser could be taken from the pencil. But after God's Son became also a human being on the first Christmas, He could never be divided into being only God or only man again. He is always both.

When we need to know how He understands us, how He is with us, how He could take our place in death, we call Him Jesus because it reminds us that He is human as we are. When we need to know that He was holy for us, that He arose from the dead, that He can take us to heaven, we use names like Lord or Christ. Then we are reminded that He is God.

But He is always both man and God. And He is always our Savior.

A Gift That Was Planned

The Word

Before the world was made, God had already chosen us to be His in Christ, so that we would be holy and without fault before Him. Ephesians 1:4a (From the Epistle for the Second Sunday After Christmas)

The World

A family heirloom gift — here is a book, but it could be an old watch, jewelry, doll, coin, etc. — wrapped as a Christmas gift with a label.

Can you guess what is in this Christmas package? I know, you've already opened your gifts, but maybe this package will have one more message to share with us about Christmas. If you feel the package, you can guess what it is. It's a book. But you still don't know which book it is. So we'll open it.

It's an old book. That is a surprise. Most of the gifts we receive are new. Think of all the new things you gave or received during the Christmas season. It seems unusual to receive a used gift. But look at the label — it is for you, from your father.

Then your father might explain his gift. The book was his when he was a child, and he kept it to give to you. Suddenly the gift no longer looks like a used book. It is something special. No one could have bought a gift like this for you. It was planned long ago — long before you were born. It tells you that your father wanted you. He thought about having children like you. The gift also shows that he wants to share something important with you. His plans to have a child turned out right. He couldn't buy this gift with money

23

or a credit card. It is something special from his own child-hood.

Our Bible reading for today says we all have received such a special gift this Christmas. The gift is from God—so you know what it is. God gave us His Son. That's what Christmas is all about. But listen to what the Bible says about the gift: "Before the world was made, God had already chosen us to be His in Christ, so that we would be holy and without fault before Him."

It says that God planned the gift of Christ for us even before He made the world. Even before Adam and Eve sinned, God loved us so much that He had a plan to keep us with Him. Christmas was not an accident. God didn't say to Himself, "Things are a mess down on earth; so I've got to think of something to straighten the place out." He knew He would give us a Savior.

God's gift to us also tells us that God planned for us to live. We are not lost people that God found. But we are God's people who got lost and were found by Him. He chose us to be His holy people. Since we are sinners, that looks like a bad choice. But notice how He chose us—we are in Christ. He gives us the gift of His Son who first makes us holy, then keeps us holy.

God planned Christmas for all people. You have received the gift. You can tell others about the gift that He also planned for them.

A Secret Is for Telling

The Word

In past times men were not told this secret, but God has revealed it now by the Spirit to His holy apostles and prophets. The secret is this: by means of the Gospel the Gentiles have a part with the Jews in God's blessings; they are members of the same body, and share in the promises that God made in Christ Jesus. Ephesians 3:5-6 (From the Epistle for Epiphany)

The World

Several party invitations, or 3×5 cards with an invitation written on them.

I'm going to let you in on a secret. See these (the invitations). They are invitations to a surprise birthday party. If a birthday party is to be a surprise, it has to be a secret, right? So I have to be careful about letting anyone see the invitations. I'll hide them here. (Put them in a book.) That way, the secret is safe.

In fact, the secret would be so safe that no one would attend the birthday party. As long as the invitations stayed hidden, no one would ever know that a party had been planned. A secret has to be told to someone sometime — otherwise there is no reason in having a secret. Something is a secret, not because it can't be told to anyone, but because it must be told to the right person at the right time.

God also has a secret. The Bible reading for today tells us His secret. It says: "The secret is this: by means of the Gospel the Gentiles have a part with the Jews in God's blessings; they are members of the same body, and share in the promise that God made in Christ Jesus."

25

That may not sound like a secret to you. You know that Christ gave the good news of the Gospel to all people. We have just celebrated Christmas when we heard again that Christ was born to be the Savior of the world. We also know what happened to Him when He died for our sins and rose again so we can all live with Him forever. None of that is a secret.

But listen to what else our Bible reading says, "In past times men were not told this secret, but God has revealed it now by the Spirit to His holy apostles and prophets." There was a time when people did not know about God's love for all people in Christ. It was a secret. And you know what — some people today still do not know the secret. They do not know God loves them. They do not know that Christ has already forgiven all their sins. They do not know that God wants them to be with Him now and forever.

But we know the secret. And God never tells us to keep the secret. We are not to hide it like I hid the invitations. Instead God tells us to share the secret — to send the invitations out. A secret must always be told to the right person at the right time. Every person is the right person because God loves everyone. Now is always the right time because we always need God's love.

Now I've told you the secret. You tell someone else.

God Found a Way to Give

The Word

You know about Jesus of Nazareth, how God poured out on Him the Holy Spirit and power. He went everywhere, doing good and healing all who were under the power of the Devil, because God was with Him. Acts 10:38 (From the Epistle for the First Sunday After Epiphany)

The World

A quart jar of lemonade (or tinted water), a bottle with a small mouth, a funnel that will fit the bottle.

This jar of lemonade and bottle can help us understand how God gives His blessings to us. If I had the lemonade and wanted to give you some in this bottle to take along on a trip, we would have a problem. It would be difficult to pour from the jar into the bottle. The lemonade would spill all over everything, and we'd have a mess to clean up.

God has a similar problem. He has many things He wants to give us. He has love, mercy, forgiveness, hope, power—to name only a few. Like this jar, God is filled with blessings He wants to share with us. But we are like the bottle. We aren't able to receive the great gifts of God. We have shut ourselves off from all of God's blessings for us.

But God still wants us to have love, mercy, forgiveness, hope, power, and all those other gifts. So He found a way to give them to us. You've probably thought of a way to get the lemonade into the bottle. Use a funnel. See, I can pour the lemonade into the funnel without spilling a drop or making a mess. Then the funnel directs it into the bottle.

God also found a way to funnel His gifts to us. He sent

us His Son, Jesus Christ, to be a part of our lives. And He poured all of His blessings into the Son. Listen to what our Bible reading tells us, "You know about Jesus of Nazareth, how God poured out on Him the Holy Spirit and power. He went everywhere, doing good and healing all who were under the power of the Devil, because God was with Him." The Holy Spirit was poured on Christ so all the gifts of the Spirit were a part of Him—all that love, mercy, forgiveness, and the rest of God's gift list for us.

But God didn't pour those gifts on Christ because Christ needed them. Christ is like the funnel—the gifts were poured into Him so He could send them on to us. He is the way we receive all of God's love, mercy, and hope.

Just as the funnel and the bottle were connected to transfer the lemonade from the jar to the bottle; so our lives and Christ are connected to transfer the gifts of God to us. Christ's birth and our birth are connected as He became one with us. His baptism and our baptism are connected as we received a new life in Him. His death and our death are connected as He died in our place. His resurrection and our future resurrection are connected as we will live with Him forever.

Study the life of Christ to see all the great blessings that God poured on Him and how He used them. Then remember He is the funnel that brings those same blessings to us, and we can also use them.

Free to Be Free

The Word

Someone will say, "I am allowed to do anything." Yes; but not everything is good for you. I could say, "I am allowed to do anything," but I am not going to let anything make a slave of me. 1 Corinthians 6:12 (From the Epistle for the Second Sunday After Epiphany)

The World

A small tricycle, a stick, small chain, piece of wire.

Christians are free. We are free because Christ has given us our freedom. He took away the problems of our sin. So now instead of being held down by fear, we are free. Christ has saved us.

If that is true, and it is, does it mean we are free to sin? If Christ has paid for all our sin, it looks like it makes no difference if we sin or not. After all, the debt of sin, no matter how big, has already been paid. Some people think that way. In our Bible reading Paul says some say they are free to do anything. Notice, those people didn't say, "I am free to sin." But claiming to be free to do anything implies I can do as I please — even if I decide to do something that is wrong.

But St. Paul tells us to stop and think about it. He agrees he is free to do anything, but then he adds, "I am not going to let anything make a slave of me." Because he remembers that he was a slave before Christ made him free, he never wants to be a slave again.

Maybe this illustration will help us understand what it means to be free. This tricycle wheel is free — see it is free to spin around. That's the way we were before sin came into the world. Then something happened to tie the wheel. (Put the chain in the wheel, and turn until the wheel is held tight.) The wheel is no longer free. That's how we were when we were slaves of sin. Then if the person who owns the trike pulls the chain out, the wheel is free again. Christ pulled the sin out of our lives; so we are free.

So now the wheel is free again—but it is free only as long as it does not get clogged up again. If a stick gets caught in the wheel, it will not be able to turn any more. Then the owner will have to free it again. If a wire gets tangled in the wheel, it will again be tied up. Again someone will have to free it.

When Christ frees us, He does not free us to sin again. Instead He makes us free to live. When we are free, we can be as He made us to be. We can be happy. We can serve Him. We can live with His people, and we can be with Him forever.

When we sin, we make ourselves slaves again because we lose our freedom. Our sin ties us down like the wheel when it was tangled up. Christ frees us over and over again in our lives. Each day we need and receive His forgiveness as He takes away the sin that we add to our own lives. But His freedom always leads us away from sin and never to sin. We want to fight against sin—not because we will go to hell, Christ has already given us heaven—because sin messes up our freedom in Him. Sin keeps us from enjoying our new life in Christ. It pulls us back to an old life again.

See the freedom God has given you. You are free to be free because Christ is in your life. Use the freedom to share freedom with others.

Something New for You to Do

The Word

What I mean, brothers, is this: there is not much time left, and from now on married men should live as though they were not married; those who weep, as though they were not sad; those who laugh, as though they were not happy; those who buy, as though they did not own what they bought; those who deal in worldly goods, as though they were not fully occupied with them. For this world, as it is now, will not last much longer. 1 Corinthians 7:29-31 (The Epistle for the Third Sunday After Epiphany)

The World

A glass of milk, a large shallow tray, a fancy guest towel.

Today's Bible reading tells us to be in a hurry to get a job done. The first sentence, by itself, would be difficult to understand. It says married people should live as though they were not married. But it also says that those who weep should live as though they were not sad, those who laugh as though they were not happy, and those who buy and sell as though they weren't interested in their business.

The Bible is not telling us not to be married, or not to be happy or sad, or not to buy and sell. Rather it says that as we live our normal lives we should remember there is something more important than the daily routine things of life.

Look at it this way: See this nice guest towel—the kind your mother would hang in the bathroom for a special occasion. She would tell you not to use the towel. It is saved for guests. Then suppose you carried this glass of milk to the living room and spilled it on the best chair. (Dump the milk

31

into the tray.) It's a mess even in the tray. Think how it would mess up good furniture.

Your mother would run to the bathroom and grab the first thing available to wipe up the mess—even if it was this nice guest towel. The towel can be washed, but it is difficult to wash a stuffed chair.

Remember the towel had a special purpose—it was kept for guests. However, in an emergency the purpose of the towel changed. It was used for something else.

The Bible reading says we also have purposes in our lives—like being married or, for many of you, being children, or laughing and crying, buying and selling. We could add to the list, but you get the idea.

Then a big event happened in our lives. We have learned that Christ is our Savior. We saw how He came to earth and showed that He was God living among us. Because we know how Christ is the Savior of not only us but also all others, God has also given us a new and more important job. We are to live with Christ in us. We who have received His blessings are to share them with others. We are to tell others the Good News that He loves them. We are to help poor people and to give love and understanding to those who are lonely and afraid.

Sure, we still have our everyday jobs too. We still laugh and cry, buy and sell. We are still parents and children. But those are now temporary parts of our lives. The big part of our lives now is that we have seen the Savior, and we have something to share with others.

Built Up by Love

It is true, of course, that "all of us have knowledge," as they say. Such knowledge, however, puffs a man up with pride, but love builds up. The person who thinks he knows something really doesn't know as he ought to know. But the man who loves God is known by Him. 1 Corinthians 8:1b-3 (From the Epistle for the Fourth Sunday After Epiphany)

The World

A small clothes basket with enough clean towels and washcloths to fill it.

Our Bible reading for today tells us two ways to decide how to do a job. One way is to use knowledge. That way says, "I know how to do the job." The other way is love. It says, "I want to do this job so that I can help others."

We'll use this basket of laundry as an example. You want to play. But your mother has said you must sort and fold all these towels and washcloths before you can go. That will take time. But if you use your brain, you can figure out a way to get it done fast. See — take a couple of towels and fold them neatly. Then place them on top, and look! The basket looks all neat and nice as though you had done the entire job. It looks right but it isn't right.

But that's not the way of love. Love doesn't make us want to look right. It makes us want to be right. The Bible reading says that knowledge puffs us up — like those messy clothes puff up in the basket to hold the few folded ones on top. But the next part of the reading says that love builds up. (Dump out the basket.) If you want to do the job to make someone else happy, you start at the bottom and build up as you fold each towel and washcloth and put them in right. (Start the job.) I won't have time to finish the job now — this way takes longer, but the job is done right.

The Bible is not telling us that knowledge is bad and love is good — both are good. You need knowledge to do the job right. I had to be able to sort and to fold — that means I used knowledge. But I used knowledge the wrong way when I tried to figure a way to look as though I had worked when I had not. All of us misuse knowledge if we use it to hurt others or to prove we are right and they are wrong.

Love is more important than knowledge because it helps direct us as we use what we know. Love doesn't look for a way to do wrong but gives us a reason for doing right.

Christ lived a life guided by love. He had all knowledge. He knew all about us. He knew our sin, our failures, everything. But His knowledge of us didn't save us. His love for us is more important. Because He loved us, He gave Himself for us so He could save us. His knowledge saw our sin, but His love paid for the sin.

We now have His love to use when we make decisions. We still use our knowledge, but as Christians we can check out what we know with how we love. Our knowledge can puff us up and make us try to look right in our own eyes and the eyes of others. But love builds us up. The love we receive makes us stronger. The love we give makes us happier.

People Can Be Adapters Too

The Word

While working with the Jews, I live like a Jew in order to win them; and even though I myself am not subject to the Law of Moses, I live as though I were, when working with those who are, in order to win them. In the same way, when with Gentiles I live like a Gentile, outside the Jewish Law, in order to win Gentiles. This does not mean that I don't obey God's law, for I am really under Christ's law. Among the weak in faith I become weak like one of them, in order to win them. So I become all things to all men, that I may save some of them by any means possible. 1 Corinthians 9:20-22 (From the Epistle for the Fifth Sunday After Epiphany)

The World

A trouble light or other electric light with an accessible bulb, a bulb, an electric radio, an adapter to screw into the light socket to make it a receptacle for the radio's plug, and a source of electricity.

The cord that comes from the electrical socket carries power to this light socket. See, when I screw the bulb into the socket it lights up. This radio also needs electricity to operate. But (take out the light bulb) the light socket has no way to provide the electricity to the radio. The power is in there. You saw it light the bulb. But I can't plug the radio into the socket. Unless, I use this (adapter). It adapts the light socket for the bulb into a socket for the plug. See. (Put the adapter into the light socket, then plug in the radio.) Using the adapter, the socket in the light can provide power for the radio. Without the adapter it can do the same for the bulb.

St. Paul, who wrote our Bible reading for today, says he

is also an adapter. The gospel of Christ has the power to save all people. Christ died for all, and He has forgiven all. But people can't receive the power of the Gospel unless it is applied to their lives. Listen to the reading. (Read the entire text.)

When St. Paul was with the Jews, he could bring the power of the Gospel to them because he also was a Jew. He understood their ways. He could show them the Savior. But the Gentiles had a different way of living. They didn't understand all of the Jewish laws. So St. Paul adapted his life to their way of living. Like putting this adapter into the socket so the plug could be used, he learned to live another way so the Gentiles could hear about Christ too.

We must also learn to use adapters in our lives. We never change the message of Christ. It is the same electricity that comes through this cord all the time with or without the adapter. But to share Christ we must understand the needs of all people. When speaking to old people about Christ, we have to use words and ideas they understand. When speaking to young people, we must use words and ideas they understand. People who haven't had the chance to go to school need the good news of Christ in words they understand. People who have good educations need the words of Christ's love and forgiveness applied to their way of thinking.

Because Christ loves you, you can be adaptable. You can understand how other people need that same message of love, and you can look for ways to share it.

Who Gets the Blame or the Glory?

The Word

Well, whatever you do, whether you eat or drink, do it all for God's glory. Just do as I do; I try to please everyone in all that I do, with no thought of my own good, but for the good of all, so that they might be saved. 1 Corinthians 10:31, 33 (From the Epistle for the Sixth Sunday After Epiphany)

The World

A number of pieces of candy (not individually wrapped) on a tray and a messy shoeshine cloth.

Everything we do is to be done so that God gets the credit. That's what the Bible reading for today tells us. It means when people see how we live they will say, "Hey, God's great." You and I know it is not easy to live in a way that God gets the glory for our lives. But because Christ is our Savior, it is possible. Let's use an illustration to help us understand how we can live to the glory of God.

Suppose my job is to advertise candy in a department store. I am to stand near the door and offer candy to kids so they will go to the candy department and buy some. But if I dropped a piece of candy on the floor, picked it up, and wiped it off with this messy cloth (do it), you wouldn't want to buy the candy. Instead of talking people into buying candy, I would be talking them out of it.

Or if I gave you the candy without telling you where to get more, I wouldn't be doing my job right. You might like the candy and think that I was a nice guy for sharing, but then I would be getting the credit. The job was to persuade you to buy candy so the store would make more sales.

Now back to our job with God. Whatever we do, even our eating and our drinking, is to be to God's glory. When we sin, we are not giving God glory. In fact when church members hate others, tell lies, refuse to help people in need, and do other wrong things, God receives blame instead of glory.

But because Christ has died for our sin, we can give glory to God even when we have done wrong. We don't have to cover up our own sin—like I tried to clean the candy I dropped and made it even worse. We can admit we are wrong and try to change. We can show we know we are forgiven by Christ and say that Christ has died for all sinners. Then God receives the glory. Other people who know they have also done wrong will know that God also offers them forgiveness. Our sin is not to God's glory, but the forgiveness is. And we can show that Christ's forgiveness has covered our sin.

We would also do our job for God the wrong way if we took credit for the good things we do. Our job is to show that God gives goodness to all people. If we take the credit, it would be like people thinking I was giving away the candy when I wanted people to go buy the candy. When others see the good works you do, the fun you have, and your faith in a God who loves you, don't let them think this is something special that you alone have. Let them know where they can receive the same joys. Send them to God. They don't have to buy anything—like the candy in the department store. God has given His love to all in Christ.

When God Says "Yes"

(Christ) is God's "Yes"; for it is He who is the "Yes" to all of God's promises. This is the reason that through Jesus Christ our "Amen" is said, to
the glory of God. It is God Himself who makes us sure, with you, of our
life in Christ; it is God Himself who has set us apart, who placed His
mark of ownership upon us, and who gave the Holy Spirit in our hearts
as the guarantee of all that He has for us. 2 Corinthians 1:19b-22 (From
the Epistle for the Seventh Sunday After Epiphany)

The World

A child's toy or pet (model plane used here. However a bicycle could
be used if the devotion is outside or, if practical, use a live pet. Change
the amount of money accordingly) and two quarters.

If you were playing in a park and saw a boy pick up this
plane, you might say, "Hey, that's a neat plane. Would you
give it to me for 50 cents?" If the other boy said "Yes,"
you'd hand over two quarters and have the plane.

But as you walked away suppose another boy said,
"That's my plane. I just flew it over in this direction and was
looking for it." He might even show you his name on it. If
you explained that you bought it, the second boy would
tell you that you had made the deal with the wrong person.
The guy who said "Yes" had no right to sell the plane. If
you make a deal with someone, make sure it is someone
who has the right to say "Yes."

The same thing is true of your deal with God. In our
Bible reading St. Paul is worried because he said to the
Corinthians, "Yes, I'll come to see you." Then he wasn't
able to make the trip. So he explained that he still wanted

to see them but couldn't. He also told them that sometimes people say "Yes" but have to break their word because they are not able to do what they say. This often happens to us. Others say "Yes" to us, then something happens so they can't do what they promised. And sometimes we say "Yes" and then have to later change it to a "No." That's why in another place the Bible says we should always say, "Yes, God willing," to show that we can't always make our own plans.

St. Paul uses his own failure to teach us something about God. He says that God never says "Yes" to us and then finds Himself unable to do what He promised. The Bible reading says, "Christ is God's 'Yes'; it is He who is the 'Yes' to all of God's promises."

God has made a deal with us. He gave us free salvation in Jesus Christ. He told us we cannot earn this gift. He gives it to us because He loves us. Because this deal comes from God, because it is His idea, we don't have to worry that we made the arrangements with the wrong person, like buying the model from the boys who didn't own it. God created both us and heaven. He makes it possible for us to be with Him. He has done this in Christ who is His "Yes" to us.

Paul says, "It is God Himself who has set us apart, who placed His mark of ownership upon us, and who gave the Holy Spirit in our hearts as the guarantee of all that He has for us."

God has said "Yes" to you. And He means it.

Who Can Do the Job?

The Word

We say this because we have confidence in God through Christ. There is nothing in us that allows us to claim that we are capable of doing this work. The capacity we have comes from God. 2 Corinthians 3:4-5 (From the Epistle for the Eighth Sunday After Epiphany)

The World

An empty picnic basket, an empty lunch box, and a brown paper bag containing a simple lunch.

If you had planned to go on a picnic and had to take your own lunch, which of these three containers would you take? If all three were on the kitchen table, would you grab the picnic basket because it is the biggest? Better check it. See, it is empty. Then would you take the lunch box? See, it's empty too. But the paper bag has a good lunch in it. See. Maybe the picnic basket and the lunch box look like they would have more food. But it is what's inside that counts. And the sack has the food.

Now make another choice. Who do you think would be the best person to tell others about Jesus? You might think that a pastor or teacher should do that job. Or you might chose someone who is older, or one who has gone to college.

But right before our Bible reading today, St. Paul says that the best messengers of God's good news about Jesus are those who have the message written in their hearts. He says not to look at the outside of a person to see how old, or how well educated a person is, or what work a person

41

does. Instead, look to see what is written in the person's heart.

Paul says he is confident that a person who has the message of Christ written in his heart can share the message because he has confidence in God through Christ. He knows Christ has given us love and forgiveness. And he knows if we have received Christ's love we have something to give to others.

The Bible reading says, "There is nothing in us that allows us to claim that we are capable of doing this work." Neither the basket, the box, or the sack have the ability to feed us. They are only containers. None of us have the ability to share God's message by our own right. No person has the ability to give eternal life to another.

But then Paul adds, "The capacity we have comes from God." God has the ability to save persons. He has done it in Christ. And He gives us the message to share. The sack could provide food because someone had put food in it. We can share the message of salvation because God has given us the message.

There are two lessons for us: First, if you want to know more about God's love for you, listen to those who share that love. Don't listen to those who only condemn or argue or find fault. Find someone who has love in them. That person will have love to give to you.

The second lesson is: You can also help do the job of sharing Christ with others. God did not chose you because you are so smart, or so old, or anything else about you. First He loved you. Now since you have that love in your heart, you have something to give to others.

A Hole in the Law

The Word

Their minds, indeed, were closed; and to this very day their eyes are covered with the same veil, as they read the books of the old covenant. The veil is removed only when a man is joined to Christ. 2 Corinthians 3:14 (From the Epistle for the Last Sunday After Epiphany)

The World

Three "veils" — pieces of heavy paper or light cardboard (heavy enough not to be opaque) at least 12 by 18 inches. Cut a hole slightly smaller than a piece of gum in one veil. Tape a piece of gum over the hole. Tape pieces of gum in the center of each of the other veils. Hold the veils so the children cannot see the gum.

The Bible reading for today tells us that some people have veils over their minds that keep them from seeing all of God's truth. I have three "veils" here, and I need three children to help us understand what the Bible is telling us. (Ask three children to come forward.)

According to our reading the problem is that the veils keep us from seeing God's grace. Since grace is seen with our heads and minds rather than our eyes; we will use a piece of gum as a symbol for God's grace. Because Christ gives His love and grace to all people, one and all, I have a piece of gum for each of you. But you have to find the gum with a veil covering your eyes. Each of you close your eyes, and I will give you a veil and help you hold it over your face. (After they have closed their eyes, give each a veil and help them hold it so it does not touch their face. The gum should be on the outside of the veils.)

Now you may open your eyes. Remember you are to look for a piece of gum, but you must not peek over, around, or under the veil. The gum is close to you. You could touch it if you could see it. When you find the gum, remove the veil. (Give the one child time to remove the gum. Let the others try for a while.)

See, one child found the gum easily. The gum was in the same place on each veil, but there was a difference. This veil has a hole in it. The child could see the gum through the hole. The others had no way to see the prize.

The Law as revealed through Moses is like a veil. It covers our eyes because it shows us that we are sinners. It makes us see only our own problems and our own faults. When we see only the Law, we either feel so guilty that we think no one can help us, or we pretend we are perfect and have kept the entire Law. In either case we are spiritually blind.

But Christ has come to help us see through the veil of the Law. He made a hole in the Law. We can look through the hole and see His love and grace. Christ's love for us has removed the threat of the Law. We don't have to pretend we are perfect. We can see our sins and yet not give up: because Christ has seen our sins and He still loves us.

We need this special view of Christ because it changes our lives. In Him we can see a new way to live. When the Law makes you afraid, remember your Savior. See the way through the Law. It is the way Christ gives you.

The Only Important Judge

The Word

Who will accuse God's chosen people? God Himself declares them not guilty! Can anyone, then, condemn them? Christ Jesus is the one who died, or rather, who was raised to life and is at the right side of God. He pleads with God for us! Romans 8:33-34 (From the Epistle for the First Sunday in Lent)

The World

A science fair project. Select one according to the age of the children present. A sea shell collection is used here. A first place ribbon.

Some of you have probably been in a science fair. You work hard on a project and, as long as it is at home, it looks great. But when you take it to the fair and you see all the other entries, your own doesn't look so good.

Let's pretend this is your science fair project. You have put it in the contest and now you notice that the shells all aren't straight. And you realize you should have had more shells. Then you see you weren't very neat. But still it's the best you could do.

You might stand back to listen to the other students and the parents as they walk by the displays. Some of the students might laugh at your entry. An adult might say, "We have a better shell collection than that." Or maybe worst of all, many people would walk by and not even notice your project.

It hurts to hear other people find fault with something you have done. You might even wish you had never entered the science fair. Then you notice the principal walk toward your shell collection. He puts a ribbon on it. You have won first prize!

Now you can forget all the bad things that others said about your project. You can forget all the faults that you saw in it. You need not remember that some people laughed at your collection. What they thought about your work doesn't count now. Even what you thought about your own project doesn't make any difference anymore. The judge thought yours was the best. It is the judge's opinion that counts.

Our Bible reading for today says that you and I are like that shell collection. Many people will find fault with us. Some will laugh at us. Others will ignore us. Many times we will even think we are no good. But the Bible says, "Who can accuse God's chosen people? God Himself declares them not guilty!" God loves you. He has said you are not guilty. He has chosen you to be His.

God did all of this when He did something very special for all people. Listen to the next sentence of the Bible reading, "Can anyone, then, condemn them? Christ Jesus is the one who died, or rather, who was raised to life and is at the right side of God. He pleads with God for us."

Christ is the one whose judgment counts. And He is the one who died and rose again so we could be free from all our faults. It is His judgment that frees us from all sin. And He gives all of us eternal life.

Is It Worth the Price?

The Word

It is a difficult thing for someone to die for a righteous person. It may be that someone might dare to die for a good person. But God has shown us how much He loves us: it was while we were still sinners that Christ died for us! By His death we are now put right with God; how much more, then, will we be saved by Him from God's wrath. Romans 5:7-9 (From the Epistle for the Second Sunday in Lent)

The World

Two birthday cards — one new, with a clean envelope, the other messy, with no envelope.

When you are shopping, you must always ask yourself one important question: "Is it worth the price?" For example, suppose you were shopping for a birthday card for your mother. You don't want to spend a lot of money just for a card; yet it would make your mother happy for you to remember her in a special way. As you looked through the birthday card rack, you might find one that looks like this (messy card). The message on the card is okay, but it is dirty and there is no envelope. The price tag says 35 cents. You may be willing to pay 35 cents but not for a card like this. Then you find another one (clean card). It is neat and clean and has a good message. The price is again 35 cents. This time you might be willing to pay the price. So you buy it.

Christ paid the price for us to be with Him forever by dying for our sins. The Bible reading for today asks the question, "Is it worth the price?" It says, "It is a difficult thing for someone to die for a righteous person. It may be that someone might dare to die for a good person." Notice what the reading tells us. If you're going to pay a high price, you want to get something worthwhile. Thirty-five cents is a lot to pay just for a card. But it is a good card; so you spend the money. Now if God is going to pay the price by sending His Son to be a sacrifice for us, you'd think He would want to make sure we were worth the price. If we were good, it might be worthwhile. But the price is too high if we are not good in His eyes.

Yet this is the miracle of God's love for us. Listen to what the text says, "But God has shown us how much He loves us: it was while we were still sinners that Christ died for us!" God saw that we were like the messed up card. He knew we lacked holiness. Yet He did not say, "Show me something else that is good and nice." He said, "I'll pay the price for sinners." God did not wait for us to become good before He would love us. He gave us His love while we were in sin.

Because God was willing to love us while we were sinners, He was also able to remove our sin. Christ's suffering and death pay the payment for our guilt. When we see the suffering and death of the Savior, we see the price God was willing to pay for us. Always remember — Christ was willing to pay the price. He didn't just get left with the bill. He gave Himself for us. It is His idea. He knows we need and can use the goodness He gave to us. He knows that through Him we can be perfect again. He thinks we are worth the price.

I'm glad He does.

Tie the Message Together

The Word

This is what it says: "God's message is near you, on your lips and in your heart" — that is, the message of faith that we preach. If you confess with your lips, "Jesus is Lord," and believe in your heart that God raised Him from the dead, you will be saved. Romans 10:8-9 (From the Epistle for the Third Sunday in Lent)

The World

A brick, rock, or heavy object about that size, and a strong string.

Do you think this string is strong enough to lift this brick? See, the string is strong. (Pull on it.) It has no cuts or weak places. The easy way to find out if the string will lift the brick is to try it. (Put the string around the brick, but do not tie it. Pull up on the string, and allow it to slip away from the brick.) That didn't prove much, did it? If we want to have a fair test, I'll have to tie the string to the brick. (Do it.) Now we test the string. See, it will lift the brick — as long as it is tied to the brick.

Now let's ask a more important question. Is the Gospel of Jesus Christ strong enough to take us to heaven? At one time or another many people face that question. When someone we love dies, or when we think we are sick or have other reasons to think about dying — then we wonder: Is all of this story about Jesus dying for our sins enough? The Bible reading for today says, "(If you) believe in your heart that God raised Him from the dead, you will be saved." However, we often would like to test that promise just like I tested the string. We need to know if the Gospel really works.

The Bible reading also tells us something else. It says, "If you confess with your lips, 'Jesus is Lord' . . . you will be saved." The message has two parts. One part is in our hearts. It tells us that Christ died and rose again. That is our faith.

The other part is on our lips. It says that Christ not only died for sins but that He died for *our* sins. It says not only that He rose from the dead but that He rose from the dead for me so I also can be raised from the dead. That is our confession of faith.

Those two parts are like the string and the knot. The string is what lifted the rock. Faith is like the string. God gives us faith to trust in Him for our salvation. By faith He lifts us from death to life. But the string of faith has to be tied to our lives. Our confession of faith—that Jesus Christ is our Lord, ties the Gospel to us. Remember God is the one who gives us the faith because He gave us the Savior, and He is also the one who ties the knot that connects us to Christ because the Holy Spirit gives us the power to confess that Jesus is our Lord.

When you hear the story of Christ's death and resurrection, see it as God dropping a string down to your life. Then see how the Holy Spirit ties the life of Christ to your life as you confess that Christ died and rose for you. Then God lifts you to a new life.

God's Way of Making a Choice

The Word

For it is by God's grace that you have been saved, through faith. It is not your own doing, but God's gift. Ephesians 2:8 (From the Epistle for the Fourth Sunday in Lent)

The World

A candy dish with one lifesaver, one piece of mashed candy, and one large candy bar. A wastebasket of junk, including the wheel from a child's toy truck and the truck with one wheel removed.

Do you have a hard time making a choice? The Bible reading for today talks about two different ways to make a choice. It says, "For it is by God's grace that you have been saved, through faith. It is not your own doing, but God's gift." God could have two ways to choose you for eternal life. One way would be to save you if you had done enough good. The Bible reading says God doesn't use that way to make a choice. The other way is by grace through faith. That is the way God has made up His mind to have you in heaven with Him.

Let's look at two ways we make choices. Then maybe we can understand God's way of choosing by grace.

First, here is a candy dish with three pieces of candy in it. If someone told you to pick any piece you want, what would you do? There is one little piece, one mashed piece, and a big candy bar. As long as you felt free to take the one you wanted, you would probably take the candy bar. You made the choice because you thought it was the best.

God doesn't make His choices that way. If He did, He

would look over the people on earth and select those who had done the least evil and the most good. They could be with Him in heaven. If He did that, He would be deciding on the basis of something in us. He would take the ones He thought were the best. That may be okay as a way to pick a piece of candy, but I am glad God doesn't use that method to choose us for heaven.

Let's look at another way to choose something. If your mother asked you to take this wastebasket out to the garbage, you might notice this wheel ready to be thrown away. You can understand why mother would toss the wheel in the wastebasket. To her it is worthless. But to you it looks valuable because you have this (the truck). See—the wheel fits on your truck and makes it a good toy again.

In this case, you choose the wheel, not because the wheel was valuable. By itself it is worthless. But it was valuable to you because you had something to use it with. Because you had the truck you could use the wheel.

God also picks us, not because we are valuable by ourselves, but because He can make us valuable. God has chosen us because there is good in Him, not because there is good in us. Because He has grace that takes away our sin, we are important to Him. Just like the wheel was important to you because you had the truck.

If God chose us by our works, He would pick some and reject others. But His grace includes us all. He offers all of us His new life because He wants us all.

Both Are the Real Jesus

The Word

In His life on earth Jesus made His prayers and requests with loud cries and tears to God, who could save Him from death. . . . When He was made perfect, He became the source of eternal salvation for all those who obey Him. Hebrews 5:7, 9 (From the Epistle for the Fifth Sunday in Lent)

The World

Several boxes, or other containers, that might be discarded by a nearby store. One box has a lid torn off, another is mashed.

The Bible reading for today shows Jesus as two different people. First it says: "In His life on earth Jesus made His prayers and requests with loud cries and tears to God, who could save Him from death." It is talking about Jesus during His life on earth when He cried out in pain, of tears, and about suffering. He pleaded with God for help. He was the one who suffered and died.

But the reading also shows us Jesus in another way. It says: "When He was made perfect, He became the source of eternal salvation for all those who obey Him." After His resurrection we see Christ ruling in heaven with the power to save all people.

In one situation Christ pleaded for help. In another, He gave help. Which is the real Jesus? If both are, and they are, how do the two different views of Jesus fit together?

Let's use this illustration to help understand. Suppose you had a friend, we'll call him Jimmy, who helped you collect things. In an alley behind a store you often found boxes like this one. Both of you liked the boxes because they are neat boxes to keep things in and to stack up in your room. You both also use them to trade with others, and you even sell some of them.

The only problem is that the people who work in the store think the boxes are no good. Sometimes they tear an end off like this. Or they mash a box like this. When you and Jimmy collect the boxes, you don't get as many as you need because some of the boxes are ruined.

Then one day Jimmy tells you he has a job at the store where you find the boxes. He is the one who opens the boxes for the store and then takes them to the alley. Because Jimmy is both the box collector and the box opener, you now know the boxes won't be torn or mashed. Jimmy can understand the problem because he collects the boxes, and he can do something about it because his job is to open them and put them in the alley.

That's why we also see Jesus in two ways. We see Him as the one who asked for help, and we see Him as the one who gives help. Christ was willing to suffer for us so we would know that He cares about us and wants to help us.

It is good for us always to see Christ in both places — as one who asked for help and one who gives help. Sometimes when we have problems, we think, or even say, "Nobody understands." Then remember that Jesus asked for help when He was in need. He understands. At other times we think, "Nobody can help me." Then remember that Christ can help. Part of the greatness of Christ is that He can do both — He was able to suffer with us, and He is also able to deliver us from suffering.

Jesus Is Lord over Death

The Word

(Christ) was humble and walked the path of obedience to death — His death on the cross. For this reason God raised Him to the highest place above, and gave Him the name that is greater than any other name, so that all beings in heaven, and on earth, and in the world below will fall on their knees, in honor of the name of Jesus, and all will openly proclaim that Jesus Christ is Lord, to the glory of God the Father. Philippians 2:8-11 (From the Epistle for Palm Sunday)

The World

A series of photographs starting with a small wallet picture to a large picture (one from a calendar will do) and a series of envelopes starting with a small envelope for an invitation, ranging to one large enough for the largest picture. Pieces of paper (the same sizes as the pictures) labeled, from small to large, blindness, deafness, diseases, demon possession, death.

Suppose your mother told you she wanted to mail these pictures to your grandmother and asks you to put them in an envelope. You might search for this envelope (small one for this picture) then another envelope for this picture until you finally found this big envelope for the largest picture. But that was a lot of extra effort. You only needed one envelope — as long as you had the right one. This one (small) by itself wouldn't do, nor would these middle-sized envelopes. But the big envelope will hold any and all of the pictures. All you need is the one big one.

We can learn something about Jesus from these envelopes. When He came to earth, He had a job to do — to save people. He met a blind man and saved him by giving him sight. (Place paper marked "Blind" in small envelope.) Blindness is a big problem for those who are blind, but not many people are blind, so Jesus was like a small envelope to many. He also met deaf people and gave them hearing. (Place "Deafness" in a larger envelope.) He cured other sicknesses—the kind that many people have. ("Sickness" is a larger envelope.) He even showed His power over the devil by casting out demons. (Use next to the largest envelope.)

But Jesus showed His greatest power in His last days on earth. Our Bible reading describes it: "(Christ) was humble and walked the path of obedience to death—His death on the cross. For this reason God raised Him to the highest place above and gave Him the name that is greater than any other name, so that all things in heaven, and on earth, and in the world below will fall on their knees, in honor of the name of Jesus and all will openly proclaim that Jesus Christ is the Lord, to the glory of God the Father."

Here Christ faced the greatest of all human problems—death. All of us eventually will die—the young and old, the sick and the healthy, the poor and the wealthy. But that is a problem that Christ can handle. (Put "Death" in the largest envelope.) Because He can die for us, He can handle all the other problems too. (Place all the other papers in the largest envelope.) You might have other worries today. But they would all be smaller than the big one—death. If we died, the other problems would be gone. Christ, who can take care of the greatest problem, can also help you with the lesser problems. Christ is Lord of all because He has died and risen again for all. He is Lord of all because He can over-rule all our problems—even death itself.

A Deathproof Guarantee

The Word

If our hope in Christ is good for this life only, and no more, then we deserve more pity than anyone else in all the world. But the truth is that Christ has been raised from death, as the guarantee that those who sleep in death will also be raised. 1 Corinthians 15:19-20 (From the Epistle for Easter Day)

The World

A child's watch and a guarantee.

When you receive a watch as a gift, there is often another gift with it that goes unnoticed. The extra gift is a guarantee. The guarantee says if anything is wrong with the way the watch was made, the company will fix it at no cost to you. It is good to have a guarantee.

Suppose you forget and leave your watch on while you soak a long time in the bathtub. Water seeps inside the watch and makes it rust. But you have a guarantee, so you take the watch back to the jeweler. But the jeweler says, "I have bad news for you. We didn't make your watch to be waterproof. The guarantee covers only our mistakes. It was your mistake to put the watch under water; so you will have to pay for it."

The guarantee was good, but it wasn't good for the problem you had. In one sense we also have a guarantee from God for our lives. We should check the guarantee to see if it covers all of our problems. God has given us our lives because He is our Creator. When we have problems, we go back to Him for help. But what if there are limits on

57

the guarantee? The Bible reading for today says, "If our hope in Christ is good for this life only, and no more, then we deserve more pity than anyone else in the world." If we think God's guarantee is only to see that we have enough to eat, and a place to live, and good health; then the guarantee won't help us in our greatest need.

Just as the watch needed to be waterproof, we need to be deathproof—that is, we need a guarantee that will cover us even if we die. If God's promises are good only until we die, then we should be pitied because no matter how healthy and well fed we are the time will come when we will die.

But the Bible reading has something else to say. Listen: "But the truth is that Christ has been raised from death, as the guarantee that those who sleep in death will also be raised." Our guarantee from God includes death also. God made us to be deathproof. He did not want us to die. But because we sinned, death became a part of our lives. But God did not cancel His guarantee. He remembers He made us to be deathproof. He sent Christ to remove our sin by dying for us. And Christ rose from the dead. His resurrection tells us that the guarantee works. Because He lives after death, we will also live after we die.

A Way to Win

The Word

This is how we win the victory over the world: with our faith. Who can defeat the world? Only he who believes that Jesus is the Son of God. 1 John 5:4b-5 (From the Epistle for the Second Sunday of Easter)

The World

A lock with key, a chain, and a sign: "Open SAT at 10 a. m."

Today's Bible reading tells us how to win a victory over a problem. To understand the way to win, let's talk about a pretend problem and ways to win it. Then we can talk about the problem mentioned in the reading.

This is the pretend problem: One of your teachers has asked you to work on a special project at school. You are to meet the teacher in your classroom at 10 on Saturday morning. Since you go to school five days a week, you know how to get there and how long it will take; so there's no problem.

However, when you arrive at the school only five minutes early, the gate is locked. I can't build the whole fence here, but you imagine a big, high wire fence with this lock and chain holding the gate shut. This sign is on the gate. It says the gate will be unlocked at 10. But you don't see anyone around to unlock it. The teacher's car is inside. So the teacher must have a key.

There are three ways to try to solve the problem. One, you could try to climb over the fence. You would hurt yourself on the wire and still not make it, but you could try. Two, you could give up and go home. After all, you tried and the gate was locked. Or three, you could believe the sign and wait until someone comes with a key to open the lock. The third choice requires that you have faith in the person who put up the sign. If that person is trustworthy, someone will come around with the key at 10, open the gate, and you can keep your appointment with the teacher.

The Bible reading suggests we take the third way. It says, "This is how we win the victory over the world: with our faith. Who can defeat the world? Only he who believes that Jesus is the Son of God."

The Bible reading is talking about a real problem — the battle against the world. This is the battle against fear and guilt, it is the battle against loneliness and evil. And the greatest part of the battle is against death itself.

There are also three ways we can fight that battle. One, we can try to win it by ourselves. We can pretend that we are really good and that we can ignore death. But we will never win the battle that way. We can only fool ourselves by thinking we are doing something.

The second way to approach the battle would be to give up. We could just quit fighting and say, "What's the use? I can't be perfect. There is no reason to even try."

Or we have a third choice. There is a sign that says, "Jesus Christ has won the battle over death for you." The sign tells us that He fought against death by dying on the cross and won the battle as He rose from the grave. We can also win the battle by faith in Him. He will unlock the doors of death and give us a new life. Our Bible reading says there is one way to win the battle — that is by faith in Christ as the Son of God. Live by that faith, and the battle is won.

Don't Hide from Help

The Word

If we say that we have no sin, we deceive ourselves and there is no truth in us. But if we confess our sins to God, we can trust Him, for He does what is right — He will forgive us our sins and make us clean from all our wrongdoing. 1 John 1:8-9 (From the Epistle for the Third Sunday of Easter)

The World

Two small boxes of coloring crayons and several sheets of paper on a clipboard.

It is always fun to get a fresh, new box of coloring crayons like this. If your teacher gave you this new box, she would probably say, "Take good care of the crayons." But it is difficult to keep crayons in good condition. (Draw boxes, circles, etc., with several of the crayons.) Just using them wears down the point. If you get interested in the picture and press too hard, the crayon will break. (Do it.) Before long, half of the crayons in the box are messed up.

Suppose the teacher asked you to put all your broken crayons out on your desk. What would you do? Since she told you to take good care of the crayons, you will have to explain how you broke some. You could just put all of yours back in the box. Then she wouldn't see how many you had broken. But you notice that some of the other kids put their broken crayons on their desk. And you know what the teacher does? She takes the broken crayons and replaces them with new crayons of the same color. After that, you quickly change your mind. If you kept your broken crayons in the box, you would miss out on the fresh, new crayons. When you put the broken ones out, the teacher takes those and gives you new crayons. (Do it.)

The Bible tells us that the same thing can happen to us and God. God wants us to be holy and good—like a new box of crayons. But we have sinned—that is like breaking the crayons. We have destroyed the goodness God gave us. Because He told us not to sin, we often try to hide from Him whatever we have in some way done wrong. But the Bible reading for today says, "If we say we have no sin, we deceive ourselves, and there is no truth in us. But if we confess our sins to God, we can trust Him, for He does what is right—He will forgive us our sins and make us clean from all our wrongdoing."

If we try to hide our sins from God, we are doing the same as hiding the broken crayons. We are keeping the problem to ourselves. We are hiding from help. But if we confess our sins, we are doing the same as placing the broken crayons out where they can be seen and replaced. God will replace the wrong things we have done with the right things Christ did for us.

Those who do not know about God's forgiveness in Christ may try to hide their sins from God. But since we know He forgives, we have no reason to hide anything from Him. When we hear the message of Christ's resurrection from the grave, we know that our sins have been taken from us. We can admit all the wrong things we have thought, done, and said. God forgives us and gives us a new life to fight against those sins.

Wait Until It's Finished

The Word

My dear friends, we are now God's children, but it is not yet clear what we shall become. But this we know: when Christ appears, we shall become like Him, because we shall see Him as He really is. 1 John 3:2 (From the Epistle for the Fourth Sunday of Easter)

The World

An unbaked biscuit (from a can of prepared biscuit dough) and a baked biscuit. A paper plate.

Would you like a biscuit now? You might be hungry for either a late breakfast or a snack before lunch. Here, I have a biscuit all ready for you (extend the paper plate with the unbaked biscuit). This is a biscuit — only it hasn't been baked yet. It is not finished yet, and it would not taste good. After it is baked, it would be like this one — and it would be delicious. If you plan to eat the biscuit, you had better wait until it is finished.

We are God's children. And in one sense we are like this unbaked biscuit. Listen to how the Bible reading for today describes us: "My dear friends, we are now God's children, but it is not yet clear what we shall become. But this we know: when Christ appears, we shall become like Him, because we shall see Him as He really is."

We are already God's children because Christ has already died for us. We have been baptized and received the new life that the Holy Spirit gives. We believe in Christ now; so we already belong to Him. But we are not yet all that we are going to be. We are like this biscuit — we aren't finished yet. God has something else to do to complete us.

The Bible reading tells us that we don't know exactly what we will become. We know that in heaven we will be different than we are here. For one thing we won't have pain and sorrow. We also know we won't sin. But there are things we don't know. We can't answer some questions about heaven because God hasn't told us some things. But we know that Christ is preparing a place for us. He'll take care of us.

The resurrection of Christ from the dead gives us the best clue about what we will be like in heaven. His victory over death is the first of many resurrections. We will become like Him. When He came to earth as a baby, He became like us. Now when we go to heaven to be saints with Him, we will become like Him.

Meanwhile, we are like the unfinished biscuit. We are not yet perfect children of God, but we are children of God. We can accept ourselves and others better when we know what we are and what we will be.

This Is What God Commands

The Word

We receive from (God) whatever we ask, because we obey His commands and do what pleases Him. This is what God commands: that we believe in the name of His Son Jesus Christ and love one another, just as Christ commanded us. 1 John 3:22-23 (From the Epistle for the Fifth Sunday of Easter)

The World

A chalkboard and chalk or a large sheet of paper on an easel and a marker pencil.

Today's Bible reading promises us something great. It says: "We receive from (God) whatever we ask." The only problem is that the sentence goes on to say, "because we obey His commands and do what pleases Him." If God gives us what we ask because we do everything He commands, we have a problem. None of us do everything that God commands.

Think of the many things that God has commanded us to do or not to do. Tell the truth. Don't hate anyone. Don't use His name in vain. Don't steal. Help people who are hungry or sick. And the list goes on and on. Maybe we can understand the commands of God better with this illustration. I need someone to help. (Choose a child old enough to do the simple math involved.) Now I will give you some commands:

Write a 1 on the chalkboard. (Let the child decide where and how big the 1 should be.) Now write another 1 beside it to make it an 11. Okay, now write a 2 under the first 1. Now another 2 beside the first 2 to make a 22. Draw a line under the 22. Put a 3 under the first 2. Now another 3 beside the first 2 to make a 33.

That was a complicated way to command you to write those figures on the board. I had to give you seven different commands. But I could have told you to do the same thing with one simple command. Let's try again: Add 11 and 22 on the chalkboard. (Let the child do it.) That was easier.

Now, back to the commands of God. Sometimes we are confused by all the commands He has given us. We know what we should do. And we know what we should not do. But we get confused by trying to remember all the possible ways we might do something wrong.

But there is also a simple way to put all the commands of God into one single command. Our Bible reading does it for us. After telling us that God gives us what we ask because we obey His commands, it says: "This is what God commands: that we believe in the name of His Son Jesus Christ and love one another, just as Christ commanded us."

Instead of telling us all the things we could do wrong and should do right, it says God commands us to believe in Jesus Christ. Because Christ has done all the things we should do and has forgiven us for all the things we have done that we should not have done, we can live under a new, simple commandment.

As people who believe in Christ, we still want to do what is right and avoid what is wrong. But now we have a way to do it. Just as a person who knows how to add 11 and 22 can decide where and how to write the problem, so we who know Christ can decide how to share His love with all other people. He gives us the love, and we can pass it on to others.

Who Owns Your Love?

The Word

This is what love is: it is not that we have loved God, but that He loved us and sent His Son to be the means by which our sins are forgiven. 1 John 4:10 (From the Epistle for the Sixth Sunday of Easter)

The World

A picture of a dog or a stuffed toy dog (in special situations you might use a real pet), a dog collar, dog dish, and some dog food.

The Bible reading for today wants to make sure we know what love is. Love is so great that no definition can be complete, but this part of the Bible tells us where love comes from. It says, "This is what love is: it is not that we have loved God, but that He loved us." It is talking about who owns the love we have. When we love God and other people, is it our love or God's love?

To figure this out, we have to talk about ownership — that is, who owns the love that brings us to God and to other people? Let's use an example: We'll pretend this picture is a real dog — not just any dog but your dog. You own him as your pet. The dog also owns some things. You would say this is your dog's collar. This is your dog's dish. And this is your dog's food. Now we are talking about double ownership. If the dog belongs to you and these things belong to the dog, do the collar, dish, and food belong to you also?

You might answer either way. You could say, "Yes, I own all the things because I own the dog." Or you might say, "No, I gave the things to the dog; so they are his." But there is one way to find a final answer. Suppose the dog lost his collar. And he chewed a hole in his dish. And he ran out of food. Who would buy a new collar? a new dish? more food? The dog? No, you would. You are the one who takes care of the dog. What the pet has comes from you. Your action is necessary for the dog to have anything.

Now let's use this idea to understand love. God has given us love. We are His children. He created us. We have love only because He gave it. He doesn't love us because we loved Him first. He doesn't love us because we have loved other people. Rather we love Him because He already loved us. We love others because He loves them and gives us love to share with them.

When we fail to love—when we hate someone—when we ignore other people; we need to receive the love that God has given in Christ. The Bible reading tells us "(God) loved us and sent His Son to be the means by which our sins are forgiven." When the dog lost his collar and dish and ran out of food, it was up to you to replace them. Even though they belong to the pet, they had to come from you. When we lose our love, we have to receive love from God through Christ. It's our love to use and to enjoy, but the love we have works only because it comes from God who loves us first.

The Spirit Makes You Sure

The Word

This is how we are sure that we live in God and He lives in us; He has given us His Spirit. And we have seen and tell others that the Father sent His Son to be the Savior of the world. Whoever declares that Jesus is the Son of God, God lives in him, and he lives in God. And we ourselves know and believe the love which God has for us. 1 John 4:13-16 (From the Epistle for the Seventh Sunday of Easter)

The World

A hinge with a removable pin. For a small group use a real hinge. For a larger group make a paper hinge, using two different colors of paper, big enough for all to easily see. Use a pencil to hold the hinge together.

Has anyone ever asked you, "Are you sure you will go to heaven?" Or have you asked someone that question? St. John talks about the problem of knowing for sure. He says, "This is how we are sure that we live in God and He lives in us." John thinks that we can be sure that God lives with us now and that we will always live with Him.

The reason we can be sure, John says, is that God has given us His Spirit. He means the Holy Spirit who brings the message of Christ to us and changes our lives. But since the Spirit can't be seen, how can we be sure? John talks about that too. Maybe this hinge will help us understand what John has to say.

See how a hinge works. It's really two pieces held together by a pin. When I pull the pin, the one hinge becomes two parts—plus the pin so that makes three parts.

Let this part of the hinge represent the life of Christ.

69

This is the entire story of Christ on earth from the time He was born, through all the things He did on earth, to the time He died and rose again. John cuts down that big, long story into one short sentence when he says, "The Father sent His Son to be the Savior of the world." For us to know that we will always live with God, we need to know that God came to live with us and for us.

But that happened a long time ago. If that's all we had, just the history of something that is 2,000 years old, we wouldn't be sure that God is with us today.

But there is another part of the hinge. This part can be called the church, if you understand that the church is the way God still gives his love to people today. The purpose of the church is to tell about the love of Christ. John talks about that job when he says, "We have seen and tell others that the Father sent His Son to be the Savior of the world." He also says, "Whoever declares that Jesus is the Son of God, God lives in him and he lives in God."

Notice how John makes sure we get the point — the church is to tell about God's love in Christ. It is to declare the forgiveness that Christ has given. But this part of the hinge by itself also has problems. Anyone can talk about love, but we need more than talk. We can say, "You are forgiven," but that is not enough. To be sure, we need to know where the love and forgiveness comes from.

That's where the Holy Spirit comes in. The Spirit connects the two other parts of the hinge. It connects the details of Christ's life with our lives today. All of those things that happened long ago happened for us. The love and forgiveness we have today is connected to the love and forgiveness that Christ brought to us all.

The Holy Spirit—Now or Later?

The Word

I will pour out My Spirit upon all flesh, and your sons and your daughters shall prophesy, and your young men shall see visions, and your old men shall dream dreams. Acts 2:17b RSV (From the Epistle for Pentecost. Use a translation that has both Old and New Testaments available.)

The World

A sack lunch containing sandwich, fruit, cookies, something to drink; a very small sack containing a dollar bill and two quarters.

There is something unusual about the verse from the Bible that we will share today. It is from Acts, that's in the New Testament. Listen to it. (Read it.) Now I will turn back to the Old Testament to Joel 2:28 and read the same words. The same sentence is in both the Old and New Testaments because Joel wrote long ago and told about something that was going to happen. On Pentecost Peter quoted Joel's prophecy and said that it had happened.

You might think it would make no difference which of the two verses we used—either from the Old or the New Testament since they both say the same thing. But each of the two verses have different meanings even though they have the same words. One says the Holy Spirit is going to come to us. The other says the Holy Spirit has come to us. The difference is important because it helps us understand the Holy Spirit in our lives today.

Looking at these two sacks may help us understand that difference. Suppose your class went on a special trip and the teacher told you to bring a sack lunch. This one will be your lunch (large sack). This one (small sack) is a classmate's lunch. You might think that the person who depended on this one (small sack) wouldn't have much to eat. But your classmate might explain the lunch this way. (Take out dollar bill.) This is for a hamburger and french fries; this (quarter) is for something to drink; and this (another quarter) is for ice cream. This one little sack offers the promise of a full meal. It will provide as much as the big sack that has a sandwich, dessert, and something to drink. The difference is that the lunch sack has the food ready to eat, but the small sack only has the money to buy the food later.

That Old Testament passage I read is like the small sack—it promises something for later. It tells the people that the Holy Spirit will come sometime in the future.

The New Testament passage is like the big sack. It says the gift has already been given. The Holy Spirit has already come to people. When we worship today, we already have the gift that God gives through His Spirit.

If we worshiped according to the Old Testament promise, we would be here to wait for the promise to be filled. But because God has already kept the promise, we are here to receive and use the power of God's Spirit in our lives today.

God's Spirit tells us that Jesus is our Savior. The Spirit fills us with faith and love as we see how Christ came into our lives to give us eternal life. The Spirit that brings Christ to us also helps us use Christ's love and power to help others. The Spirit moves us to tell others about Christ. The Spirit helps us see other people as Christ sees them and to help them as Christ helps them.

Our worship today is not just a promise from God what He will do in the future and then a promise from us about what we will do in the future. The Holy Spirit is God's gift to us now. And we can use His power now.

A God Who Does It All

The Word

The grace of the Lord Jesus Christ, the love of God, and the fellowship of the Holy Spirit be with you all. 2 Corinthians 13:13 (From the Epistle for the First Sunday After Pentecost)

The World

A lunch tray with a sandwich, something to drink, and a piece of pie.

The Bible reading for today is the New Testament benediction. The word benediction means a "good saying." A benediction not only says something good about God, but it also says the good is for us. This benediction says, "The grace of the Lord Jesus Christ, the love of God, and the fellowship of the Holy Spirit be with you all."

The benediction could have just said, "God's grace, love, and fellowship be with you all." It would mean the same because Christ is also God and the Holy Spirit is also God. The idea of a Trinity, that is, one God but three persons is often confusing to us. Why not just say God and keep it simple?

One reason for speaking of God as a Trinity is that it helps understand the good things that God has for us. Not only do we have God's grace, but we can understand that grace because God's Son, Jesus Christ, became a person like us to pay for our sins and to give us eternal life. When we give the good words of grace through Jesus Christ, we are not just talking about a good idea but about grace that Christ has earned for us.

When we speak about the love of God the Father, we

73

know it is a special love—not only the love that made Him create us but the love that He continues to give us even though we are sinners. And the fellowship of the Holy Spirit tells us that God's Spirit works in all of us to bring us together in Christ.

Of course, we can say that God is great. And that is true. But we can see how His greatness is shared with us and how it changes our lives when we see how God has given us His grace, love, and fellowship in the persons of the Trinity.

Maybe this illustration will help. This is a lunch. (Show the tray.) I can tell you what a good lunch it is. It is delicious, and it will be good for you. But the easiest way for me to make you know how good the lunch is would be for me to show you the parts of the lunch. Instead of just talking about the lunch, let me show you this sandwich with lots of meat and fresh bread and all the right trimmings. Then here is something to drink, cool and refreshing. And for dessert, a piece of fresh, homemade pie with real fruit and a flaky crust.

All of this makes a good lunch. But you can know the lunch is good by knowing about each part of the lunch. This is not a perfect example of the Trinity since the lunch is divided into three parts, and we can't divide God three ways. There is one God, but we can see and appreciate His blessings for us when we see how we are blessed by the Father, Son, and the Holy Spirit.

Now let's hear the good words of that benediction again: "The grace of the Lord Jesus Christ, the love of God, and the fellowship of the Holy Spirit be with you all."

Know What You Are Judging

The Word

For it is not ourselves that we preach; we preach Jesus Christ as Lord, and ourselves as your servants for Jesus' sake. . . . Yet we who have this spiritual treasure are like common clay pots, to show that the supreme power belongs to God, not to us. 2 Corinthians 4:5, 7 (From the Epistle for the Second Sunday After Pentecost)

The World

An attractive (and, if possible, expensive) vase with a wilted flower and a plain clay flower pot containing a beautiful plant.

If you were the judge in a flower show and you had to pick between these two entries, which would you take? It's an easy choice. This flower is wilted and dead. This one is alive and beautiful. In a flower show, this one wins.

But what if you were the judge in a contest for the best flower container? That's a different contest. This beautiful flower is in a plain, cheap clay pot. The pot does nothing except hold the beautiful flower. This vase is beautiful. Even though the flower in it now is nothing, the vase is beautiful all by itself. (Take the flower out.) It would look nice on your table even without the flower.

If you are to be a judge, you have to know what you are judging. If you judge flowers, this one wins. If you judge containers, this one wins.

In our Bible reading St. Paul tells us how to judge people who tell you about Christ. He says, "For it is not ourselves that we preach: we preach Jesus Christ as Lord, and ourselves as your servants for Jesus' sake. . . . Yet we who have this spiritual treasure are like common clay pots, to show that the supreme power belongs to God, not to us."

If someone tells us about Christ, we can judge one of two things — either the message, or the person who gives us the message.

If we judge the person who gives the message, then we look for someone who has a nice sounding voice and speaks in a way we like. We judge one speaker better than the other because we like the way the one looks or sounds.

But if we judge the message, then we listen to what is said. We listen to hear the message of God's love for us in Jesus Christ. We want to see how Christ's life for us has given us God's grace and how our lives are different because Christ is our Lord.

The Bible reading says we should be concerned about the message not the person who gives the message. The person who gives the message is only a container. He is like the clay pot, not much in itself, but it contains something beautiful.

There are two lessons for us in this Bible reading. First, always listen for the message of Christ rather than someone who impresses you by his or her way of speaking. The other message is also important: You can tell others about Christ. You need not be a great speaker. You need not have people say, "That was a great talk." Instead you should speak so people will say, "That was a great message." Then you have chosen and they have found the right message.

Something New in Something Old

The Word

For this reason we never become discouraged. Even though our outward nature is decaying, our inward nature is being made new day after day. 2 Corinthians 4:16 (From the Epistle for the Third Sunday After Pentecost)

The World

A small decorated cardboard box and a supply of cookies.

Most children are hungry when they come home from school or playing. One mother who had to work and could not be home when her child came home found a nice way to always have a snack ready. She fixed this pretty box. Every morning she put something in it for the child's snack. In the afternoon when the child came home, a snack was always ready in the box.

In the weeks that followed, the box began to show some wear and tear. One time the lid got torn. (Do it.) The decorations fell off. (Remove them.) Some things were spilled on the box that made it messy.

Do you think the child complained about the box? No, there were no complaints because each day the mother put in a fresh, new snack. (Do it.) The child didn't worry about how the box looked as long as the snack was there.

Today's Bible reading says our physical bodies are something like this box. Listen: "For this reason we never become discouraged. Even though our outward nature is decaying, our inward nature is being made new day after day."

When God created us, He gave us fresh, new bodies like this box was before I messed it up. Our bodies are fine

77

gifts from God. But through the years we get pains and scars. Though you young people might not have noticed it yet, you are already starting to grow old. We should take good care of our bodies, but even if we do, our bodies will still become old and weak.

That makes some people afraid and unhappy. They think they are losing their lives when their bodies start to wear out. But the Bible reading says we don't have to be discouraged. Even though our body is wearing out, we have a new life in us that is made new every day.

When God made us, He not only gave us a physical body, but He also gave us a soul for our spiritual life. Our spiritual life would also become sick and worn out if we had to live with our own guilt and sin. But Christ is our Savior. He has taken away all the wrongs that would damage our spiritual life. Each day we receive new spiritual strength from Him. Even though our bodies grow older each day, our spiritual life remains fresh and new because the Holy Spirit continues to give us His new life.

We are like the box that contained a fresh new lunch each day. Even though our bodies grow old and wear out, we will continue to receive the new life in Christ. Therefore we do not have to be discouraged or afraid because something goes wrong with our physical body. The new life in us will continue even when we die, and we will be raised to live with a new and glorious body.

What You Believe Is What You Get

The Word

For our life is a matter of faith, not of sight. 2 Corinthians 5:7 (From the Epistle for the Fourth Sunday After Pentecost)

The World

A small, undeveloped fruit or vegetable and a mature fruit or vegetable of the same kind. (Or a flower bud and a full bloom may be used.)

Have you heard the expression, "What you see is what you get"? In many cases that statement is true. When you look at the grades on your report card, you can say, "What I see is what I get." Or if you complain about the food on your plate at dinner your mother may say, "What you see is what you get."

But there are other times when the statement is not true. Suppose you had a garden with a cucumber plant. If you went out to look at the vines and saw this little cucumber, you could say, "What you see is what you get." That would mean you might as well pick the little cucumber because that's all that you are going to get.

But I'd like to suggest another expression for the cucumber and for you. It is, "What you believe is what you get." If you believe the little cucumber will grow, then you can leave it on the vine until it becomes a big cucumber like this one. Of course, something could happen to kill the cucumber vine, or the fruit might fall off, but if you believe the little cucumber will grow and if you are right, then you will have a big cucumber. But if you follow the "What you see is what you get" idea; you will pick it when it is small.

Today's Bible reading tells us how to make a choice in our lives between the "What you see" and the "What you believe" ideas. It says, "For our life is a matter of faith, not of sight." Suppose we disagreed and said that our life is what we see. That would mean, "What we see is what we get." And we see many nice things in our lives. We have food, clothing, family, homes — all the things we see in our lives. But if our life is only what we see, we are not receiving all the gifts that God gives. He has given us what we see, but He has given us much more. He says our real life is more than what we see — it is what we believe.

The Bible reading says our life is a matter of faith, not sight. What we believe is what we get. When we believe in Christ, we receive Christ. When we believe He forgives us, we have forgiveness. When we believe He loves us, we are filled with love. When we believe that even though He died He still lives, we receive a new life.

Remember your life is not just what you see but also what you believe. Enjoy the gifts you see that have been given by God. But they are not the greatest gifts He has for you. They are temporary — just for now. What you believe in Christ is for now and forever.

How to Blow Out Death

The Word

For we are ruled by Christ's love for us, now that we recognize that one man died for all men, which means that all men take part in His death. 2 Corinthians 5:14 (From the Epistle for the Fifth Sunday After Pentecost)

The World

A handful of small balloons, one large balloon, a candle, matches.

Today's Bible reading tells us that Christ died for all people. Then it says that we all take part in His death. Because He died a long time ago, it might seem impossible for us to share in His death. Yet we do. Maybe these balloons can help us see how we take part in His death.

Pretend the balloons are people. God creates us and gives us life. (Blow up first balloon.) My breath in this balloon is like the spirit that God our creator puts in us. You can't see the spirit, but it changes our lives. However, we have sinned. (Tie the end of the balloon.) Tying the balloon is a sign of our sin. Now I can no longer breathe more air into the balloon. When we sin, we cut ourselves off from God. (Blow up several balloons and tie them.)

When we do wrong, we must be punished. The punishment of sin is death. This candle will be a symbol of death. Its flame stands for the punishment of sin. Each person must go through death. (Bring the balloon near the flame so it breaks the balloon and the flame is extinguished.) Death paid the price of sin by putting out the flame, but it also destroyed the balloon. If we must pay our own punishment for sin, our life will be destroyed.

But Christ became a human like us. This balloon (large one) will represent Christ. He also became a person living on earth. (Blow up the balloon.) Only Christ did not sin so the end is not tied. Even though Christ had no sin, He offered to die for us. But Christ could approach death in a different way. (Place the end of the balloon near the flame and allow air to escape the balloon and extinguish the flame.) See death was destroyed, but Christ was not. He could face death and win the battle.

Now we share in that victory. When we face death, Christ is with us. (Light the candle again and place a small balloon and the Christ balloon near the flame. Again let the Christ balloon blow out the flame) We can pass through death because Christ is with us. Death cannot destroy us. (Repeat with several other balloons.)

Because Christ is not separated from God by sin, He continues to receive and use the power of God. (Blow up the Christ balloon again.) His resurrection gives Him an eternal life that He shares with us.

When you think of your own death or the death of anyone else, think of the two balloons together by the flame. Christ will be with you when you die. Christ is with others. He can blow out death.

You Can Give Because . . .

I am not laying down any rules. But by showing how eager others are to help, I am trying to find out how real your own love is. For you know the grace of our Lord Jesus Christ; rich as He was, He made Himself poor for your sake, in order to make you rich by means of His proverty. 2 Corinthians 8:8-9 (From the Epistle for the Sixth Sunday After Pentecost)

The World

A dollar's worth of change, a pitcher of lemonade, two glasses.

Suppose this is your allowance (the dollar's worth of change) for a week. It is one dollar, but all in change. How much of it do you think you should give to the church or to help other people? Should you give a penny? or a dime? or a quarter? Today's Bible reading helps answer that question.

Notice I said it *helps* answer the question. The Bible doesn't tell you how much you have to give. St. Paul, who wrote the reading for today, says, "I am not laying down any rules." He can't decide how much you should give. Instead he gives you two examples to follow.

The first example is Jesus. St. Paul reminds us, "For you know the grace of our Lord Jesus Christ; rich as He was, He made Himself poor for your sake, in order to make you rich by means of His poverty."

To illustrate how rich Jesus is and how He shares His riches, let's use this pitcher as a symbol of God. It is filled with lemonade — that is a symbol for a full, rich life. God is filled with riches to give to us. But we are like this empty glass. But our sin has made us far away from God. We have refused the life He has for us. But Christ became a glass like us. Only He was without sin; so He could receive the riches of God. (Pour lemonade into the second glass.) Christ was filled with the new life, and He gave His life for us so we could have His riches. (Pour from the Christ glass into the other empty glass.) Through Christ we have the riches of God. Christ died to give us this gift, and when He rose from the grave, He was made rich again. (Refill Christ glass from the pitcher.) So we can have life with Him.

That's one example. It tells us that when we have gifts from God we can give them away because we know God will continue to give His gifts to us. Christ could give His life away because He knew His life would return.

The other example is the Christians from Macedonia. When they heard the Christians in Judea were poor and hungry, the Macedonia Christians sent food and money. St. Paul says, "By showing how eager others are to help, I am trying to find out how real your own love is." He wants us to see how other Christians gave their money to help others. They are an example for us to follow.

We still haven't told you how much of your dollar to give. St. Paul says not to give because there is a law that tells you how much to give. Instead give because you want to give. Give because you know how Christ has given His life for you. And give because you know you can help others.

When God Says "No"

The Word

Three times I prayed to the Lord about this, and asked Him to take it away. His answer was, "My grace is all you need; for My power is strongest when you are weak." 2 Corinthians 12:8-9a (From the Epistle for the Seventh Sunday After Pentecost)

The World

A soft drink in bottle or can, several paper cups (one with a large hole in its bottom, another with a small hole on its side near the bottom so it cannot easily be seen and two cups with no holes) and a large shallow pan.

Why does God say "no" to some of our prayers? We know God loves us. He loves us so much He has given His Son to be our Savior. His love has taken care of the big problem—our sins are forgiven, and we are going to heaven. But we still have other problems. We get sick, we have temptations, we are afraid, we fail. Why doesn't God solve those problems too?

Today's Bible reading tells us why God sometimes says "no" to us. St. Paul had asked God to take away one of his problems and God said "No." And God told him why. He said, "My grace is all you need, for My power is strongest when you are weak." Paul already had God's grace. And the power of that grace was stronger when Paul remembered his need for God's grace.

This illustration might help. Suppose you are visiting a friend and the friend's mother says you can divide this soft drink. So you can divide it, she gives you these paper cups (the two with holes). Then she tells you that some of the cups have holes in them and asks you to check so you won't lose your drink. Your friend looks at his cup (the one with the big hole) and sees a hole in the bottom. His mother gives him a different cup—one with no holes. You look at your cup (the one with a small hole), and it looks OK. So you divide the drink. (Pour into both cups while they are in the shallow pan.) Your friend drinks from his cup. But look at yours. (Lift it up.)—It did have a hole, and your drink is running out.

Because your friend's cup had a big hole, he knew he had to get a new cup. The hole in your cup was so small you didn't see it and thought it was OK. See, the mother had another cup with no hole in it, but you didn't ask for it.

For the same reason God sometimes has to let us keep a problem. When we have a problem, we know we need His help. If our problem is obvious, like the cup with the big hole, we know we need God's grace and ask for it. But if we think we can handle our own problems, we are like the cup with the small hole. Then we keep on living with the idea we don't need help when we really do.

God says "yes" to most of our prayers. But when He does say "no," He is not angry at us, and He is not forgetting us. Instead He is letting us keep a problem as a reminder that His grace is enough for us. If we think we are strong by ourselves, then we might think we didn't need Him. But when we know we are weak, then we know we need His help. His power is the strongest in our lives when we recognize our own weaknesses.

Do You Know Where to get Forgiveness?

The Word

For by the death of Christ we are set free, and our sins are forgiven. Ephesians 1:7a (From the Epistle for the Eighth Sunday After Pentecost)

The World

A balloon in the pocket of another person present such as an usher, parent, or any person known by the child involved, and a coupon that says, "Good for one free balloon." If practical you might have a coupon and certificate for every child present. Candy or another gift can easily be substituted for the balloon.

I have a gift certificate here for Cindy. Cindy, would you please come and get it. It says, "Good for one free balloon." That certificate, which is all yours, is not a joke. There is a balloon reserved for you.

But you have one problem. This certificate tells you what you will receive — a balloon. It also tells you the price — free. But it doesn't tell you where to get the free balloon. The gift certificate is worthless to you until you know where to get it. If you don't know what to do with it, you'd have to throw it away. So I'll tell you. Cindy, that usher has your balloon in his pocket. If you give him the certificate, he will give you the balloon.

Now I have another certificate for all of you. It is from our Bible reading for today. The reading says, "Our sins are forgiven." You and I have forgiveness. Everything we have ever done wrong is forgiven. All the wrong things we have said are paid for. Even our evil thoughts and sins we don't know about are wiped out. You have forgiveness. And it is free.

But do you know where to get that forgiveness? Just words don't assure us of forgiveness. Our sins are real and the payment must be real. Forgiveness isn't ignoring sin. Forgiveness isn't hiding sin. Forgiveness means someone pays for our sin. Do you know where to go to get the forgiveness?

I think you do know, but to remind you I want to read the rest of the Bible reading for today. It says, "For by the death of Christ we are set free, and our sins are forgiven." When we need forgiveness, we know where we can go to get it. We go to Christ. He is the one who paid for our sin. He is the one who gives us forgiveness.

You can go to Christ for forgiveness because He has come to you. He came to you in your baptism as He gave you a new life. He comes to you each time you hear His message of love and eternal life. He comes to you to give you power to love others and to share your forgiveness with them.

Going to Christ does not just mean going to church; though you do receive His message here. But you can take that message with you. Everywhere you go, Christ is with you. He is the one who continues to give you God's love and forgiveness.

The Walls Come Tumbling Down

The Word

For Christ himself has brought us peace, by making the Jews and Gentiles one people. With His own body He broke down the wall that separated them and kept them enemies. Ephesians 2:14 (From the Epistle for the Ninth Sunday After Pentecost)

The World

Six large blocks from a set of children's toys (pieces of 2×4's or milk cartons may be used) and two small dolls or stick figures.

Christ breaks down the walls that separate us from one another. That's what our Bible reading tells us. To understand how Christ takes down the walls, we must also understand how and why we build up the walls.

Let's go back to the reasons people build walls of separation. This (a doll) is you and this (other doll) is a neighbor. A long time ago you might have noticed your neighbor was collecting many arrows and spears. He said he needed them to hunt animals, but you got worried. So you built a wall to protect yourself. (Put up a wall of three blocks in front of the first doll.) But the other guy saw your wall and wondered what was going on behind it. He thought you had even more weapons. So he built a wall too. (Use other three blocks.) People who had been neighbors became enemies.

Today we have different kinds of walls, and we build them for different reasons. If you see another person who has more money, or gets better grades, or has more friends than you, you may build a wall between you and that person by saying you don't like him. Your wall is made of jealousy. The other person will feel your wall of jealousy and build his own to protect himself from you. Or another person may hurt you by hitting you or saying something bad about you. You get angry and build a wall of hatred to protect yourself from being hurt again. Or we can build walls of ignorance and prejudice between us and other people who are from different races or live in different places. Some build walls between themselves and others, between those who are older or younger, poorer or richer. We have many reasons to build walls.

But Christ came to take the walls down. He loves all people and brings us together. Now notice how He does it. He starts by taking down our wall. (Take down the blocks by the first doll.) We would like for Him to start with the other guy's wall. However, Christ always comes on our side of our own walls to help us. He helps us see we need not be jealous, we don't have to hate, we don't have to be afraid. We are free from all those things because He is our Savior. Since He has taken away our guilt, we don't have to protect ourselves from others. We don't have to prove we are right. We don't have to think we are better than others. We don't need walls to defend ourselves because Christ has defended us. If He is for us, who can be against us?

Christ defends us, not by destroying our enemies but by removing our walls. He offers to do the same for those who build walls against us. Sometimes others want to keep their walls. But no matter, we need not keep ours. We have Christ to protect us; so we don't need those walls.

Think about the walls that separate you from others. Don't just see the walls that others have built. See first your own walls and see how Christ removes them. When you have the faith to live without the walls that separate you from others, the others may feel free to come out from behind their walls too.

The Tie That Holds Us Together

The Word

Do your best to preserve the unity which the Spirit gives, by the peace
that binds you together. There is one body and one Spirit, just as there
is one hope to which God has called you. There is one Lord, one faith,
one Baptism; there is one God and Father of all men, who is Lord of all,
works through all, and is in all. Ephesians 4:3-6 (From the Epistle for the
Tenth Sunday After Pentecost)

The World

Five keys and a key chain, five people and a rope or heavy cord about
ten feet long and with the ends tied together.

If you had to carry these five keys, it would be easy to
lose some of them. The best way to keep them is to get a key
chain. (String the keys on the chain.) Now all the keys are
together, and the chain will keep them together.

Today's Bible reading tells us the Holy Spirit is like a key
chain, and we are like the keys. The Spirit holds us together.
Listen and notice how often the number one is mentioned:
"Do your best to preserve the unity which the Spirit gives
by the peace that binds you together. There is one body and
one Spirit, just as there is one hope to which God has called
you. There is one Lord, one faith, one Baptism; there is one
God and Father of all men, who is Lord of all, works through
all, and is in all."

I also have one rope here, and it represents all the one's
in the reading. It is the one God, one faith, one Baptism. I also
need five people to help me. (If possible select a child, a teen-
ager, an older person, a male, a female, and as many races

as represented. If the group has only children of one race, ask them to play the role of older people and other races.)

Even though you are all different, not only in the way you look but also different as individual people, you can all be held together by one power. Each of you hold on to the rope. Remember this rope is the one God who created each of you. Each of you believes in Jesus Christ as your one Savior. When you are with Christ, you are with all other people who believe in Him because there is one body of believers. Each of you have been baptized by one Baptism; therefore you all share the one new life in Christ.

Here you can see the unity you have with each other because you are all holding the same rope. But the invisible rope of the Holy Spirit that holds us all together reaches far beyond this room. It includes all people around the world who know Christ as their Savior. It reaches back into time to our ancestors who knew Christ, and it reaches forward into time to those who will come after us and who will also worship Jesus.

St. Paul tells us to preserve the unity we have. Don't let go of the rope to get away from others who also believe in Jesus. Don't go away to do your own thing, but stay close to the Spirit that holds us together.

What If You Learned the Wrong Way?

The Word

In the Lord's name, then, I say this and insist on it: do not live any longer like the heathen, whose thoughts are worthless, and whose minds are in the dark. . . . That was not what you learned about Christ! You certainly heard about Him, and as His followers you were taught the truth which is in Jesus. So get rid of your old self, which made you live as you used to—the old self which was being destroyed by its deceitful desires. Ephesians 4:17-18a, 20-22 (From the Epistle for the Eleventh Sunday After Pentecost)

The World

A dart board with several darts.

If you learned to play darts with a friend who told you that if a dart landed here (in a corner outside the ring) you got to throw it again, you would think that was the right way to play the game. From then on when you played (put several darts in the corner areas) and this happened, you would go get the darts and throw them again. (Do it.) However, that is not the right way to play darts. The rules say that if a dart lands in this area you get five points off your score.

Since you learned to play the game the wrong way, you would have trouble every time you played with someone else. You might even insist that your way was right. That could cause an argument and ruin the game. If you insisted that the wrong way was the right way, you would have trouble each time you played. You would have to change your way of thinking and remember the right way to play.

Our Bible reading tells us we have learned the wrong way

to live and we need to change. It says, "In the Lord's name, then, I say this and insist on it: do not live any longer like the heathen, whose thoughts are worthless, and whose minds are dark." We have learned to be selfish, proud, and greedy. We have learned to hate, steal, and lie. And sometimes we even think that we should live the wrong way. When we do that, we are playing the dart game with the wrong rules.

Our Bible reading offers help. It says, "That was not what you learned about Christ! You certainly heard about Him, and as His followers you are taught the truth which is in Jesus." In Christ we have found a new way to live. We can love instead of hate, we can help others instead of being selfish. We can be kind instead of being mean. But that means we have to be willing to change our way of thinking. We have to recognize that we learned to do some things the wrong way, and in Christ we can learn the right way.

The Bible reading tells us how to learn the right way. It says, "So get rid of your old self, which made you live as you used to — the old self which was being destroyed by its deceitful desires." Jesus gave us a new life so we can get rid of the old life. Our new life learns to live from Christ so we can get rid of the old ways that we learned from other sinners.

Trade Off the Bad for Good

The Word

Get rid of all bitterness, passion, and anger. No more shouting or insults! No more hateful feelings of any sort! Instead, be kind and tenderhearted to one another, and forgive one another, as God has forgiven you in Christ. Ephesians 4:31-32 (From the Epistle for the Twelfth Sunday After Pentecost)

The World

A piece of spoiled fruit (a peeled apple left unprotected looks spoiled in a short time) and a fresh piece of the same fruit. A new pair of socks and a single sock with holes in the toe and heel.

Would you want to eat this apple (spoiled one)? If it was the only thing you had to eat, would you trade it for this one (fresh apple)?

Or look at this old sock. I can't call it a pair of socks because one is lost. And this one has a hole here and another here. But if that were the only sock you had, you might say it was better than none, but not much better. What if someone offered to trade you this brand new pair of socks for the one old sock?

Trading something bad for something good looks like a rip-off for the one who gives away the good and receives the bad. But the trade is great for the one who gives away the bad and receives the good. Yet the Bible reading for today offers us such a good trade. It tells us we have something bad, like this spoiled apple or worn-out sock, that we can trade for something good, like the fresh apple or new pair of socks. Listen to the reading: "Get rid of all bitterness, passion, and anger. No more shouting or insults! No more hateful feelings of any sort! Instead, be kind and tenderhearted to one another, and forgive one another, as God has forgiven you in Christ."

When you are bitter or angry, you hurt others. And you also hurt yourself. Being angry keeps you from enjoying life. When you are angry, you can't see all the good things in life, but you see only those things that make you more angry. A person who is bitter is not fun to be with.

So why not trade away your bitterness and anger? Don't keep them. Don't hide them away for later. But trade them off for a new way of living. The reading says that instead of bitterness and anger you can be kind and tenderhearted. Christ offers to make this trade with you. He will take your anger and bitterness because He is willing to pay for all wrong. He will give you kindness. He will make you tender-hearted.

Or think of another trade. Do you shout bad things at others to insult them? Do you have hurtful feelings against others? When you insult someone else, you are saying as much against yourself as you are against the other person. When you call someone else a bad name, others hear the bad name on your mouth. Why not trade off those hurtful things. Trade them for forgiveness. As Christ has forgiven you, you can forgive others.

People who have kindness and forgiveness are happier than those who keep their bitterness and hurtful feelings. They are closer to God, and they get along better with other people. Why not make the trade now?

Use Your Gifts Wisely

The Word

So pay close attention to how you live. Don't live like ignorant men, but like wise men. . . . Don't be fools, then, but try to find out what the Lord wants you to do. Ephesians 5:15, 17 (From the Epistle for the Thirteenth Sunday After Pentecost)

The World

A can of fruit (metal can), a can opener, and an ice pick.

The first sentence of today's Bible reading has good advice for us all. It says: "So pay close attention to how you live. Don't live like ignorant men, but like wise men." All people do some ignorant things once in a while. All people do some wise things once in a while. How are you doing in your life?

The difference between the two is obvious. Suppose I wanted to eat the fruit in this can. First, I have to open the can. One way would be to make holes in the top with this ice pick. If I made some holes, I could pour out the juice. If I made enough holes, I could get the lid off and eat the fruit. Of course, I need something to pound on the ice pick. I could use this (can opener). See, I can use it like a hammer to drive the ice pick through the lid. But that is the ignorant way to do something. If I have a can opener, I should use it to open the can (do it), rather than as a hammer to punch holes in the can.

Now let's apply this idea of using something the right way or the wrong way to our spiritual lives. The Bible reading tells us to pay close attention to how we are living in our relationship to God. Are we using His gifts in a wise way?

God has given us many things. He has given us our bodies, minds, and feelings. We have eyes, ears, voices. We have money, time, and abilities. We sometimes use these things the wrong way. The Bible reading says, "Don't be fools, then, but try to find out what the Lord wants you to do." It is foolish to use God's gifts the wrong way. The gifts will work the wrong way just as the can opener could be used as a hammer to drive the ice pick. But that wasn't the wise way to use the can opener. And the wise way to use all of our gifts from God is to use them the way He planned. We can use our voices to say kind and helpful things instead of mean, hurtful things. We can use our eyes and ears to understand people and find ways to make others happy rather than to find fault with them.

You think of other wise and foolish ways you can use God's gifts. Because we are sinners, we will misuse God's gifts. But even then God gives us help. We can use his help in a wise, not foolish, way. His help came to us when Jesus came to be our Savior. Jesus gave us God's love and forgiveness.

We use Christ's love and forgiveness in a wise way when we know we are forgiven for what we have done wrong and that God will help us do what is right. The foolish way to use God's love is to think that God doesn't care if we sin. God does care because He does love us. Sin hurts us and God doesn't want us to be hurt. So pay close attention to how you live. Use Christ's love to help you live your life wisely.

The Clue of the Cross

The Word

Wives must submit themselves completely to their husbands, in the same way that the church submits itself to Christ. Husbands, love your wives in the same way that Christ loved the church and gave His life for it. Ephesians 5:24-25 (From the Epistle for the Fourteenth Sunday After Pentecost)

The World

Make a puzzle from a sheet of heavy paper. Draw a large cross on one side (side A), and let the other side (side B) blank. For young children, cut the puzzle in a few simple pieces; for older children make it more complicated. Pin the pieces, side B up, at random on a large piece of cardboard, and hold the cardboard upright so others can watch as you work the puzzle.

Have you ever tried to put together a puzzle like this? Notice that it has no picture. It is difficult to find pieces that match because there is no picture to give clues. But if I turn the pieces over (do it), the puzzle is easier to put together. (As you turn the pieces to side A, also start to assemble it.) Now I have clues to show how the pieces fit together. See, the picture is a cross. The cross is a reminder that we have a Savior who won a victory over death for us.

Just as the cross gave us clues on how to put the puzzle together, it also gives us clues about how we are to live with one another. In one way people are like the puzzle with no picture. (Turn several of the pieces back to side B.) Often we don't know how we fit with other people. Brothers and sisters, husband and wives, parents and children, teachers and students have a difficult time knowing how they are to live with one another.

But Christ helps us find the right way to live together. When Jesus came into our lives, He turned us over. (Turn all pieces back to side A.) When Jesus is in my life and your life, He shows us how we belong together. (Illustrate with two pieces of puzzle that each have a part of the cross.)

The Bible reading for today tells how Jesus helps a husband and wife live together. Even though you may not get married for a long time, this reading shows the kind of love you can share with a husband or wife sometime. It also can help you understand how you fit together with others now. It says: "Wives must submit themselves completely to their husbands, in the same way that the church submits itself to Christ. Husbands, love your wives in the same way that Christ loved the church and gave His life for it."

Often we are afraid to love someone with a total love — with the kind of love that says "I give my life to you and would die for you." But Christ gives us that kind of love. Because we have that love from Him, we can give it to others. The love of Christ keeps people together when their human love is weak or fails. The love of Christ is the clue that shows us how to live with others. Each of us can remember that we belong to Christ so He will help us give and receive love. And we remember that others belong to Christ so we will accept their love too.

Check Your Anger

The Word

Remember this, my dear brothers! Everyone must be quick to listen, but slow to speak, and slow to become angry. For man's anger does not help to achieve God's righteous purposes. James 1:19-20 (From the Epistle for the Fifteenth Sunday After Pentecost)

The World

A lead pencil, clipboard with paper.

Today we are going to talk about a problem that most of us have. The problem is — getting angry. Sometimes we call it "getting mad," but angry is the proper word even though we use both words to mean the same thing. We should know the difference between hating someone and being angry with someone. It is always wrong to hate another person. But we can and do get angry at people we love. In fact, most of the times we are angry, our anger is at someone who is close to us.

Anger is not always sinful. In one place the Bible says, "If you become angry, do not let your anger lead you into sin" (Eph. 4:26). We know that Jesus became angry at those who turned God's temple into a place to cheat others. Yet anger is often a problem for Christians. Often when we get angry, we do sin by saying hurtful things to or about others. And we must remember that Christ's anger is not an excuse to defend our own anger. He was holy and used His anger the right way. Today's Bible reading warns us that we often use ours the wrong way. It says, "Remember this, my dear brothers! Everyone must be quick to listen, but slow to speak, and slow to become angry. For man's anger does not help to achieve God's righteous purposes."

Anger causes many problems. For one thing an angry person seldom hears what others say. In case we are wrong, our anger only makes us more wrong because we can't hear the other side. Also an angry person says things he would not ordinarily say. When we get angry, we often say things that make others angry at us. So the Bible reading tells us to be quick to listen and slow to speak when we are getting angry. Listening more and talking less helps keep anger in control.

This lead pencil can help us understand the problem of getting angry. The pencil is a way for us to get a message to another person. With it I can write something for you to read. But if I want to make the message stronger, I press down on the pencil. See — now the words look louder. But if I press too hard, I will break the lead. (Do it.) Now I can't write at all. When we speak in a normal voice, people listen to us. Sometimes we start to get angry and raise our voice. More may listen for a little while. But if you get too angry, no one will listen. It is like breaking the lead in the pencil. You have lost the way to share your message.

Our reading tells us: "Man's anger does not help to achieve God's righteous purposes." When you start to get angry, remember Christ will help you. He does not help by telling you to hide your anger. Hiding your anger makes the problem worse because you keep it inside and use it on the wrong person. Instead Christ helps to keep you from getting angry. He reminds you He loves both you and the person you are angry with. He will help you both listen and speak in a way that shows this love. Remember the problems that anger can cause, and let Christ take those problems from you.

Choose the Right Way to Choose

The Word

My brothers! In your life as believers in our Lord Jesus Christ, the Lord of glory, you must never treat people in different ways because of their outward appearance. Suppose a rich man wearing a gold ring and fine clothes comes in to your meeting, and a poor man in ragged clothes also comes in. If you show more respect to the well-dressed man and say to him, "Have this best seat here," but say to the poor man, "Stand, or sit down here on the floor by my seat," then you are guilty of creating distinctions among yourselves and making judgments based on evil motives. James 2:1-4 (From the Epistle for the Sixteenth Sunday After Pentecost)

The World

Cut out the following shapes and colors of paper: Three small disks (red, green, and yellow), three large disks (same three colors) two small triangles (red and green), one large triangle (yellow). Secure all the pieces to a cardboard with straight pins.

Kent, I want you to help me. See all the pieces of paper on the board? I am going to choose one. And I want you to pick all the pieces that match the one I pick. You are to take as many as you can. Here is a little, green disk.

(Let the child make the decision. Discuss the choices with him, and let the hearers in on the discussion. Start by being selective and choose as few as possible. If he takes all green papers, he will have only three. If he chooses by size, he should have five since there are two small triangles. If he takes all circles by choosing shape, he would get six.)

Notice that if Kent selects by color he gets only three,

103

by size he gets five, and by shape he gets six. But there is one way for him to have all nine of the pieces. Kent chose the pieces that are made of the same material as the one I gave you. See — they are all made of paper. So if you match the one you have with the others according to what it is made of, you get all of them.

Now let's imagine that all these pieces of paper on the board are people. People also come in different sizes and shapes and colors. There are young and old, big and little, male and female, black, white, red, and yellow. And Jesus also became a person. He came to be the Savior. But what kind of people did He save? If we say that we are to match other people with Him to find out who is saved, who will we pick? Just men, because Jesus was a man? Or just Jews because Jesus was a Jew? Or just holy people because Jesus never sinned? No. Jesus came to be the Savior of everyone. He was a real person. So all people match Him. Christ died for all people. You are included. And everyone else can have this gift too.

Then when we choose people, we are to use Christ's way of making the choice. We don't just choose good people because we know Christ loves all people. We don't just select people from our own country or our own race, because Christ loves all people. When you look at all these pieces of paper, you can see how they are different. But you can also see how they are alike — they are all paper. When you look at people you will see their differences, but also remember to see that Christ loves each of them. Listen to what our Bible reading for today says. (Read the entire text.)

Faith That Changes Life

The Word

My brothers! What good is it for a man to say, "I have faith," if his actions do not prove it? Can that faith save him? Suppose there are brothers or sisters who need clothes and don't have enough to eat. What good is there in saying to them, "God bless you! Keep warm and well!" — if you don't give them the necessities of life? This is how it is with faith! If it is alone and has no actions with it, then it is dead. James 2:14-17 (From the Epistle for the Seventeenth Sunday After Pentecost)

The World

Two large glass bottles or pitchers filled with water, a red button, red food coloring, several water glasses.

Jesus Christ is your Savior. That means He has saved you from sin and from hell, and He has saved you to do good things for Him and for others and finally to be in heaven. When you have faith in Jesus, you know you don't have to try to save yourself because He has already done it for you. Faith is important because it receives Christ's work for us. Let's look at two illustrations of faith and see which one describes how we believe in Jesus.

This bottle of water represents you. Now I will add something to the water. (Drop in the red button.) The red represents faith. It is added to your life. You have faith. The faith is there and can be seen, but notice it is seen in only part of your life. Even though the red button is in the bottle with the water, it has not changed the water. See, when I pour out water into a glass (do it), the water is the same as it was before the red was added. In your life, if faith has not changed what you do, it is a dead faith. You can say you have faith, like this bottle has a red button, but unless the faith changes each part of your life, it is a dead faith.

Today's Bible reading says: "My brothers! What good is it for a man to say, 'I have faith,' if his actions do not prove it? Can that faith save him? Suppose there are brothers or sisters who need clothes and don't have enough to eat. What good is there in your saying to them, 'God bless you! Keep warm and eat well!'—if you don't give them the necessities of life? This is how it is with faith: if it is alone and has no actions with it, then it is dead."

We need another illustration of faith. Now this second bottle is your life. We again add red. (Pour in red food coloring and shake the bottle.) This time the red changes all parts of the water. Now when I pour out some of the water, the red coloring is included. Living faith is the same in our lives. When we believe in Christ, our faith changes everything we do. It is a part of what we say. It is shown in how we treat other people and how we spend our time and money. Our words and actions pour out part of our lives to others like pouring from this bottle into glasses, (Do it.) The water poured into the glass is different because the red is in it. Our words and actions are different because Christ is in them.

Check your faith. Is it like the first bottle—something you have that has not changed your life? Is your faith just saying words without doing what the words say? Or is your faith like the second bottle? Is your faith living because the Christ who lives in you is living? The Holy Spirit gives us a living faith.

Know What Comes with Your Feelings and Actions

The Word

For where there is jealousy and selfishness, there is also disorder and every kind of evil. But the wisdom from above is pure, first of all, it is also peaceful, gentle, and friendly; it is full of compassion and produces a harvest of good deeds; it is free from prejudice and hypocrisy. James 3:16-17 (From the Epistle for the Eighteenth Sunday After Pentecost)

The World

Six boxes of cereal. On the back of each box put one of the following words printed in large letters: Wisdom, peaceful, gentle, friendly, compassion, good deeds. Six soap boxes with the following on the back: Jealousy, selfishness, disorder, all kinds of evil, prejudice, and hypocrisy.

Suppose you are in the grocery store to buy a box of corn flakes. If you saw this box (soap), you would know you were in the wrong aisle. If you kept looking in the same place, you would only find more soap. (Put all the soap boxes out.) But when you found this box (cereal other than corn flakes), you would know you are close. So you would keep looking (putting out other cereal boxes) until you found the one you wanted. Cereals and soaps come in boxes about the same shape and size. But what is in the boxes is different. No store manager would mix them up. (Do it.) That would confuse the customers. Instead they are kept in separate parts of the store. (Separate the boxes again.)

Today's Bible reading talks about our feelings and actions.

In some ways we have two sets of feelings and two ways of behaving just like I have two kinds of boxes here. To help us understand the Bible reading, I have words on the backs of these boxes. (Turn the boxes around.) You watch these words while you listen to the reading: "For where there is jealousy and selfishness, there is also disorder and every kind of evil. But the wisdom from above is pure, first of all, it is also peaceful, gentle, and friendly; it is full of compassion and produces a harvest of good deeds; it is free from prejudice and hypocrisy."

Notice that James, who wrote the Bible reading, says our feelings and actions are separated into two groups like the soap and cereal. He says where there is jealousy (point to it), there is also selfishness and disorder and all kinds of evil. Later he says prejudice and hypocrisy belong in this group too. But he also says where there is wisdom, we also are peaceful, gentle, friendly, full of compassion and produce a harvest of good deeds.

Because we are sinners we feel and do the things in this group (soap). Because Christ is our Savior, the Holy Spirit has given us the things in this group (cereal). We should know that we can't mix the two groups. If we take just one from this group (soap) and mix it with the other (do it), the others will come along too. (Mix them all.) Where you have one, you will have the others.

But the reverse is also true. If we have one of this group (cereal), it will help us have the others. The gifts of God are stronger than the others. Christ has won a victory over all of these kinds of feelings and actions. (Separate the soap boxes again.)

When you choose, your feelings and your actions know which group you are selecting. Remember if you pick one from either group, the others will come along with it. These are the feelings and actions (cereal group) that give us joy and happiness.

What Will You Run Out of First?

The Word

And now, you rich people, listen to me! Weep and wail over the miseries that are coming upon you! Your riches have rotted away, and your clothes have been eaten by moths. Your gold and silver are covered with rust, and this rust will be a witness against you, and eat up your flesh like fire. James 5:1-3a (From the Epistle for the Nineteenth Sunday After Pentecost)

The World

A yardstick, a tape measure with the ends tied together, a handful of coins, a handful of small pieces of cloth, cellophane tape.

Today's Bible reading tells us that being rich might make us miserable. Listen: "And now, you rich people, listen to me! Weep and wail over the miseries that are coming upon you!" You know that having money often makes many people happy. And those who are unhappy often think that more money would make them happy. Yet James, who wrote the text, explains why money might make us unhappy. He says, "Your riches have rotted away, and your clothes have been eaten by moths. Your gold and silver are covered with rust, and this rust will be a witness against you, and eat up your flesh like fire."

This illustration may help us understand why riches can make us miserable. I have a handful of money here and a handful of little pieces of cloth to represent clothing. Suppose this yardstick is your life. You were born here (at beginning of the ruler), and now you are about here (at 10). You need money and clothing. The Bible reading doesn't say such things aren't necessary. (Tape a coin and a cloth at 10.) As you grow older, you will need even more. (Tape coins and cloths along the tape until about 26.) One way that riches could make you unhappy is for you to run out of them. If money and what it buys are the only things that make you happy and you lost your money, you would have no reason to be happy. Then you would be miserable.

But the solution is to have more money. Have enough to last until the end of your life. (Put a number of coins and cloths at the end of the ruler.) If you die rich, you will never have to worry about running out of money. But then you have run out of life—so your money and clothes won't make you happy any more. Either way—if you run out of money or you run out of life—money can't keep you happy. Trusting in money and what it buys can make you miserable because it only gives temporary happiness.

But Jesus has a different way for us to live. Our life is like this (tape measure). We need money and clothing. (Tape on some of each.) But if we have neither, our life goes on. (Keep pulling the tape through your hand, allowing the knot to pass through so the children can see it is continuous.) In Christ you never run out of life. He has given you His life. Even when you die, you will continue to live in Christ because He died for you. And He rose from the grave so you can live with Him. You can use and enjoy the gifts God has given you such as money and clothes. But even if you run out of those things, you will not run out of life. He has given you a way to have happiness that lasts.

We Are All Covered with the Same Holiness

The Word

(Jesus) makes men pure from their sins, and both He and those whom He makes pure all have the same Father. That is why Jesus is not ashamed to call them His brothers. Hebrews 2:11 (From the Epistle for the Twentieth Sunday After Pentecost)

The World

A can of red paint (or any bright color but not black or white), a paint brush, several different blocks of wood (as many shapes and sizes as practical, old but not rotten), a large cloth or piece of plastic.

All of these blocks are alike in one way. They are different shapes and sizes and have a variety of color. But they are all wood. I want to compare us, that is, you, me, and other people, to these blocks of wood. We are different in many ways, but we are also alike in many ways. We are all human beings. And we are all sinners. The fact that we are sinners makes us alike, but it doesn't make us like each other. Our sins make it difficult for us to live with each other.

There is one way to make all of these blocks of wood alike in another way. Watch! (Put the blocks on the paint cloth, and paint them with the brush. Continue to paint as you talk.) This can of paint is red. When the brush is dipped in the paint, it becomes red. Notice that the blocks now look like they belong together. They have also become red. They match each other, and they match the paint in the can and on the brush.

God has also given us a new way to be like each other. Instead of being the same because we are sinners, we can be the same because we are saints — that is, we can be holy people. And holy people can live together and like it.

God is like this can of paint — only He is filled with holiness. For today pretend that holiness is red. Christ brought that holiness to us just as the brush carried the red paint to the blocks. As the blocks are covered with red paint, we are covered with Christ's holiness. Notice that His holiness not only makes us like Him but also like each other.

Remember how Christ gave God's holiness to us. He died to take away our sins. He suffered because we were wrong. The holiness that He gives us does not just cover our sins like this paint covers the blocks. Christ removes our sins. He gives us His goodness instead.

Our Bible reading for today tells us: "(Jesus) makes men pure from their sins, and both He and those whom He makes pure all have the same Father. That is why Jesus is not ashamed to call them His brothers." We cannot give ourselves holiness. Our holiness would be the wrong color. It would not be like God's. It would not be like other people's holiness. But we have been made pure by Christ. All the goodness we have comes from God; so we match Him. And we match others who also receive their goodness from God.

The blocks were just pieces of wood before, but now that they are painted they have become a set. They belong together. When we have the new life in Christ, we also are changed. God is not ashamed of us. He is proud of us. He loves us and wants us to stay with Him and with each other.

The Word at Work

The Word

For the Word of God is alive and active. It cuts deeper than any double-edged sword. It goes all the way through, to where soul and spirit meet, to where joints and marrow come together. It judges the desires and thoughts of men's hearts. Hebrews 4:12 (From the Epistle for the Twenty-first Sunday After Pentecost)

The World

A scissors and four sheets of paper (large enough for everyone to read the words) with a large circle in the center of each. One of the following pairs of words on each sheet (the first word outside the circle, the second inside), hate, love; greed, generosity; lies, truth; unbelief, faith.

Each Sunday we read a section of God's Word. The reading for today tells us about itself. It says: "For the Word of God is alive and active. It cuts deeper than any double-edged sword. It goes all the way through, to where soul and spirit meet, to where joints and marrow come together. It judges the desires and thoughts of men's hearts."

First, remember that God's Word is like a two-edged sword. I don't have a sword, but this scissors also has two edges. See, one blade of the scissors would be like a knife. (Show one blade while covering the other with your hand.) The two blades work together to cut. The two messages of God's Word also work together to cut deep into our thoughts. One blade is like God's law—it shows us we are sinners. The other blade is like God's Gospel—the good news that Christ our Savior and our sins are forgiven.

Next, remember a scissors won't cut until it is used. God's

Word must also be used in our lives. The reading says God's Word is alive and active. (Open and close the scissors.) The Word works in our lives. The reading says it cuts down deep into our lives. It judges our desires and thoughts and separates them deep inside our lives.

These papers show some of the thoughts and desires that are in our hearts. We have both love and hate (show paper), greed and generosity, lies and truth, unbelief and faith. And God's Word cuts deep down into our lives to the point where these thoughts come together. (As you talk, cut out each circle by cutting through the outside word and around the circle. Throw away the outer paper.)

Notice how the scissors cuts at the point where the two blades and the paper meet. When God's law and the Gospel meet in our lives, we can cut away the hate, greed, lies, and unbelief. The Law blade helps us see our sin, and the Gospel blade says the sin is removed. The Word of God cuts away the bad in our lives and brings out the good. The good is a gift from God. Our love is no longer hidden in hate. Generosity is not covered by greed. Truth not destroyed by lies. Faith not clouded by unbelief. The Word of God is like a two-edged sword that brings the power of Christ into our lives.

Each time you hear God's Word, see it as the two edges of the scissors. Let it cut to the place you need help. If you have pride, let the Law help you see it and remove it and the Gospel of Christ move you to share any God-given talent. Put all the problem areas of your life right at this point where the Law and the Gospel work together in your life. Then your thoughts and desires are judged by Christ Himself. And the one who judges also forgives. He makes you a new and free person.

A Priest with Something to Give

The Word

Every high priest is chosen from among the people and appointed to serve God on their behalf. He offers gifts and sacrifices for sins. Since he himself is weak in many ways, he is able to be gentle with those who are ignorant and make mistakes. And because he is himself weak, he must offer sacrifices not only for the sins of the people but also for his own sins. Hebrews 5:1-3 (From the Epistle for the Twenty-second Sunday After Pentecost)

The World

A large sack of candy and four small plastic sacks — one containing five pieces of candy, another four, another three, and another two.

Suppose you were selling candy for trick-or-treat gifts. Each sack is to have six pieces of candy. But look at this one — it has only two pieces. And this one has only three. Here's one with four. They can't be sold that way if the customer is paying for six pieces of candy.

In one way we are like these sacks of candy. We are not filled with goodness. God created us to be holy — filled to the top with good deeds. But on Judgment Day we would have to be put aside just as these sacks would have to be put aside when they should have been sold.

But our Bible reading tells us that a high priest has been appointed to help us. It says: "Every high priest is chosen from among the people and appointed to serve God on their behalf. He offers gifts and sacrifices for sins. Since himself is weak in many ways, he is able to be gentle with those who are ignorant and make mistakes."

115

Since a high priest was chosen from the people, we will choose this sack (one with five pieces) from among the sacks to help the others. This sack can make gifts to the others to help them pass the test. If I take two pieces from this sack and put them in this one (with four), it will pass; and three pieces to this one so it will pass. But now there is a new problem. The sack that gave help to others is empty. It isn't ready for sale. In fact, if you kept count you know this sack had only five pieces of candy in it at the beginning, so it was never ready to be sold. It needed help itself and couldn't help others. Our reading also says, and because "he (that is, the high priest) is himself weak, he must offer sacrifices not only for the sins of the people but for his own sins."

None of us can be high priests to pay for the sins of others when we cannot even pay for our own sins. But Christ came to be our high priest. He is like this big sack of candy. He gives the gifts that will make us all pass the test. (Put six pieces of candy in each small sack.) Because Christ is holy there is no limit to the holiness He gives us. Even this big sack would eventually be empty, but Christ will never run out of goodness for us. And because He also became a person with us, He is gentle with us and understands our mistakes.

Because Christ is the high priest who pays for our sins and makes us holy, we can also be priests to one another. We can also be gentle and understand how others are weak and sinful because we are the same. Even though we can't pay for someone else's sins, we can tell others about Christ who has given help to everyone.

116

Believe and Be Sure

The Word

For we have heard the Good News, just as they did. They heard the message, but it did not do them any good, because when they heard it, they did not receive it with faith. Hebrews 4:2 (From the Epistle for the Twenty-third Sunday After Pentecost)

The World

A soft-drink bottle filled with water and capped, the soft drink poured in a plastic container (the kind used to store leftovers—small enough to be completely filled). Wrap both the bottle and the container in tissue paper.

I need a volunteer to help me explain the Bible reading for today. Karen, will you help? (Select a child at least eight years old.) Would you like to have a soft drink? (Name the brand or flavor.) I have one for you. It is in one of these packages. But notice both are wrapped. You may feel them, but you may not peek inside the paper. Before you choose, let me make a suggestion. The soft drink is in this package (the small one).

(Let the child make the choice. Be prepared for either possibility. If she takes the one with the water, let her open it and see what is in it. Then open the other and show her the soft drink. If she takes the smaller one, let her open and drink it. Alter the following explanation to apply to the child's choice.)

That was a difficult choice because your eyes told you the soft drink would be in the package that looked like a bottle. Yet I told you the drink was in the smaller package. The real question was: Would you believe your eyes or would you believe me?

The Bible reading for today says we have the same choice about the good news of Christ. Listen: "For we have heard the Good News, just as they—that is, people in the Old Testament—did. They heard the message, but it did not do them any good, because when they heard it, they did not receive it with faith." The reading is talking about people in the Old Testament who would not believe God. He told them they could live in the Promised Land. But their eyes told them the people in the land had a large army. So they believed their eyes instead of God, and they never lived in that great land that God planned for them.

The Good News mentioned in the reading is the news that Christ is our Savior. It tells us God loves us and gives us eternal life with Him. It says we don't have to earn His love and that when we die we will be raised from the dead. Some people can't believe the good news of Christ. They think they have to earn everything they get. They think that dead people will stay dead. Because they do not believe the message of Christ, they will not receive the gift God has for them.

But I tell you the message so you will believe it. Christ is your Savior. I believe that. I know He died and rose again for me and that He died and rose for you. At times our eyes will tell us to believe something else. But remember the Good News comes from God. You can believe Him. Just as I knew what was in these packages because I wrapped them, God knows what is in eternal life because He got it ready for you.

We Don't Have a "Throwaway" Priest

The Word

There is another difference: those other priests were many because they died and could not continue their work. But Jesus lives on forever, and His work as priest does not pass on to someone else. And so He is able, now and always, to save those who come to God through Him, because He lives forever to plead with God for them. Hebrew 7:23-25 (From the Epistle for the Twenty-fourth Sunday After Pentecost)

The World

A package of tissues and a clean handkerchief.

Our Bible reading for today is about priests; so maybe we had better define the word. A priest serves as a go-between for God and people. A priest gives the people a message from God. A priest prays to God for people. In the Old Testament there were many priests. In the New Testament we are told that all Christians are priests. All of us deliver a message from God to others. All of us pray not just for ourselves, but we also pray for others.

The Bible reading tells us that Jesus Christ is a special priest. It says, "There is another difference: those other priests were many because they died and could not continue their work. But Jesus lives on forever, and His work as priest does not pass on to someone else. And so He is able, now and always, to save those who come to God through Him, because He lives forever to plead with God for them."

Let's compare ourselves as priests to this tissue. (Remove one tissue from the pack.) As priests we have a job today.

119

A tissue has a job to do. If you have a cold, you use it to blow your nose or when you sneeze. Or you may use it to wipe your eyes if you are laughing or crying. The tissue may be used to clean your face or to wipe up dust. But no matter how you use the tissue, you will throw it away. Tissues come in packs because after they are used they are thrown away. (Pull out several.) But now look at this handkerchief. It can be used for all the same jobs that the tissue is used for. But there's a big difference. You don't throw away the handkerchief after you use it. Instead it is washed and ironed and used over and over again.

If we are like the tissues, Jesus, our special priest, is like the handkerchief. The reading says there are many regular priests because we die and cannot continue to work as priests. Christ died as a priest because His death was a sacrifice for us — He gave Himself. Yet He continued to work as a priest. He came back to life. He still lives now. He is still our priest. We don't have a throwaway priest. We have an eternal priest who is able to save us. Just as the handkerchief can get dirty and messy and then be washed clean, Christ took our sins on Himself, then rose from the dead with a clean, new life. And He gives us that new life.

We still need human priests. We need someone to tell us about Christ, and we need to tell others. We need to pray for others and to have others pray for us. But our being priests depends on the special priest, Jesus Christ. He is the one who will also be priest for everyone.

Remember, This Is Jesus' Second Visit

The Word

Christ also was offered in sacrifice once to take way the sins of many. He will appear a second time, not to deal with sin, but to save those who are waiting for Him. Hebrews 9:28 (From the Epistle for the Twenty-fifth Sunday After Pentecost)

The World

A glass vase, pieces of glass that look like they could be the vase broken, several quarters, and a ten-dollar bill.

I am going to tell you a story, and I want you to pretend it is about you. It is your birthday, and your grandmother is coming to visit you. She lives faraway and doesn't come to see you often. You have to go to school on your birthday, but you know your grandmother will be there when you come home.

Sounds like a great birthday, right? But there is a problem. On her last visit your grandmother left a special vase at your house. And after she had gone, you were looking at it and you dropped it. This (the broken glass) is all that is left of her vase. You will have to show her these pieces and then buy a new vase for her. You have this much money (the quarters) to give her now, and you promise to keep a quarter out of your allowance each week until the vase is paid for. So instead of being excited about seeing your grandmother, you dread telling her the bad news.

But when you get home, she is not there. Now you have to wait to face her. When she comes she says, "Look, what

I have" (the vase). She explains that when she came to your house while you were at school she discovered the broken vase, so she went out and bought a new one. Instead of paying for it one quarter at a time, like you planned to do, she used this (ten-dollar bill) and bought the vase. Now, you and your grandmother can celebrate your birthday without worrying about the vase. The broken vase can be thrown away and forgotten because it has been replaced and paid for.

That pretend story is a parable about a true story—a true story about you. Our Bible reading tells the story when it says, "Christ also was offered in sacrifice once to take away the sins of many. He will appear a second time, not to deal with sin, but to save those who are waiting for him."

Breaking the vase is like our sin. We have broken God's law by doing wrong. And God has told us that He will come on Judgment Day. We may think we can pay for our sins by trying to do good like trying to pay for the vase one quarter at a time in the story. But yet we know that when Christ comes we will not have enough to pay for all our wrong.

But like grandmother in the story, Christ comes to us twice. First He came to see our sin and pay for it. The Bible reading says He didn't pay a little at a time, but in one sacrifice, when He died on the cross, He paid for all sin.

Now when Christ comes on Judgment Day, He is not coming to deal with sin. All sin has been paid for. Instead He is coming to celebrate with us. He has saved us, and we can live with Him forever. When you think about Jesus coming to the world, remember this is His second visit.

A Ticket from God and to God

The Word

Every Jewish priest stands and performs his services every day and offers the same sacrifice many times. But these sacrifices can never take away sins. Christ, however, offered one sacrifice for sins, an offering that is good forever and then sat down at the right side of God. Hebrews 10:11-12 (From the Epistle for the Twenty-sixth Sunday After Pentecost)

The World

A real ticket to a local theater (or place of entertainment that children in the area could attend) and the following written on a 3×5 card: "Admit one to (name of place)."

Our Bible reading for today tells us about two kinds of sacrifices. Remember a sacrifice was used to pay for sins. In the Old Testament and at the time Jesus lived people would kill a sheep, calf, or other animal as an offering, a sacrifice for sin. The reading says, "Every Jewish priest stands and performs his services every day and offers the same sacrifices many times. But these sacrifices can never take away sins."

Even though the sacrifices didn't really pay for their sins, they kept trying. In one way a ticket to a movie is like a sacrifice because it pays your way to the theater and a sacrifice pays your way into heaven. Suppose you had this ticket (the 3 × 5 card) to a theater. It says: "Admit one to . . . ." If you took the ticket to the theater, the usher wouldn't let you in. The ticket is no good because it didn't come from the theater. I wrote it, and I can't tell the usher to let you in. If you did try using this fake ticket and it didn't work, would you keep

123

on trying to use it? Once you know it is a fake, you might as well throw it away.

That's why we don't offer animal sacrifices for our sins. Giving animals didn't pay our way; so why do it? But we have to ask ourselves the same question if we keep repeating other ways to pay for our sins — other ways that also do not work. Do you try to do more good things than bad things with the idea that the good will somehow make God forget the bad? Do you go to church, pray, or give money with the hope that such things will pay for sin. There are reasons to do such good things, but none of them pay for sin.

But our Bible reading tells us about another kind of sacrifice. It says, "Christ, however, offered one sacrifice for sins, an offering that is good forever and then sat down at the right side of God." Christ gave Himself, not animals, to pay for sin. And His one sacrifice did the job even after thousands of other sacrifices had failed. His sacrifice worked because He came from God to be our Savior, and after He paid the sacrifice, He went back to be with God.

Christ's sacrifice is like this ticket (real one). If you take it to the theater, you can get in to see the movie. The ticket is good because it came from the theater, and you will take it back to that theater to use it.

When you see your sin, think of Christ as the sacrifice who paid for your wrongdoings. Remember the good you do cannot pay for the wrong you have done. But the good Christ has done for you came from God; therefore it is a sacrifice that has paid your way to be with God. Take the goodness Christ gives you as your ticket from God to God.

How Can Jesus Give Us So Much?

The Word

God has raised from the dead our Lord Jesus, who is the Great Shepherd of the sheep because of His death, by which the eternal covenant is sealed. Hebrews 13:20 (From the Epistle for the Twenty-seventh Sunday After Pentecost)

The World

A checkbook, a pen, and a deposit slip.

The Bible reading for today calls Jesus the Great Shepherd. You've seen pictures of Jesus taking care of sheep. The Bible never tells us that He worked as a shepherd. Jesus may have worked as a carpenter. He may have worked on fishing boats. But we don't know that He ever took care of a sheep.

But when we call Jesus the Great Shepherd, we aren't talking about sheep. He is the Shepherd who takes care of people. Jesus gives us everything we have. He gives us love, hope, forgiveness, mercy, and all the other gifts in our spiritual life. Other gifts such as food, home, family, clothes are also gifts from Jesus though they come through other people. Jesus is the Great Shepherd who provides for us.

In fact, it might seem that saying everything comes from Jesus is too simple. Why do we give Him credit for giving us all the good things in life? Maybe this illustration will help: Do you recognize this (a checkbook)? It is a checkbook. There are many kinds of checkbooks, but they all contain blank checks like these. You have seen your mother or father write out checks to pay their bills. It looks so simple to see them pay every bill. All they need is the blank check and a pen, like this, and they can write out checks to pay all the bills. If it is that simple, then why not buy more things? After all, it is easy to write checks to pay the bills.

I hope you know why it is not so simple to pay bills with checks. You need more than checks and a pen. You also need this (deposit slip). It is a deposit slip. Your parents have to put money in the bank with the deposit slip before they can write a check. Then they can't write checks for more money than they have deposited.

Jesus also had to make a deposit for us so He could be the Great Shepherd who provides for us. The Bible reading tells us about His deposit. It says, "God has raised from the dead our Lord Jesus, who is the Great Shepherd of the sheep because of His death, by which the eternal covenant is sealed."

Jesus gave Himself for us. He died to seal a covenant— that means to keep a promise. The promise was that He would save us and He did. All of His gifts for us come from the deposit He made for us just as all checks your parents write must come from the deposits they made. Jesus can give us forgiveness because He died to pay for our sins. He can make us holy because He deposited His holiness for us. He can give us hope and eternal life because He rose from the dead and lives with us now.

When you hear about all the gifts the Great Shepherd gives you, don't see just the gifts like checks because you might forget how valuable the gifts are. Also see the deposit slip of Christ's death for you so you will know the gifts are real.

Watch for the Light You Saw Before

The Word

Look, He is coming with the clouds! Everyone will see Him, including those who pierced Him. All peoples of earth will mourn because of Him. Certainly so! Amen. "I am the Alpha and the Omega," says the Lord God Almighty, who is, who was, and who is to come. Revelation 1:7-8 (From the Epistle for the Last Sunday After Pentecost)

The World

A slide or filmstrip projector (or a strong flashlight) and three poster-size pieces of paper each with one of the following messages: "Who is," "Who was," and "Who is to come."

I have asked Tom, Sara, and Bruce to help me explain the Bible reading for today. Let's start by looking for the light in this projector. (Turn it on.) Do you know where the light is? (Turn the light off, and help the children find the light bulb inside the case. If practical, open the case to show the bulb.)

But it's not the bulb in the projector that's important. The light that comes out of the projector is the light that makes pictures on the screen for us. Let's use the light that shines from the projector to help us understand the Bible reading. First, listen to it: "Look, He is coming with the clouds! Everyone will see Him, including those who pierced Him. All peoples of earth will mourn because of Him. Certainly so! Amen. 'I am the Alpha and the Omega,' says the Lord God Almighty, who is, who was, and who is to come."

The Bible tells us about Judgment Day when Christ will come to judge the world. All the dead will be raised, and all people will see Him when He comes. Tom, take this poster and stand by that wall. (Shine the light on the poster.) The light of God will show us the one who is to come. We will all see Him.

But God wants us to recognize Him when He comes to judge us. He will not come as a stranger. We will know Him because He has been here before. Sara, take this poster ("Who was") and stand near the front of the projector. (Have the poster about one-third of the distance from the projector to the other poster. Shine the light on the second poster.) See, the same light shines on this poster as on the other. God says He is both Alpha and Omega — that is, the first and last letter of the Greek alphabet. He is A and Z, the first and the last. God who is going to come is the same God who created the world. The same God who loved us and sent His Son to die for us. The same God who raised Christ from the grave to give all of us a victory over death so we could live forever. Just as we have seen God in the past, we will see Him in the future. (Shine light from one poster to the other.) And He is the same God.

But God also says He is the one who is. Bruce, take this poster ("Who is") halfway between the other two. (Shine the light on the last poster.) God also is with us today. Today He loves us. Today He forgives our sins. Today He comforts us and guides us. Today He invites us to follow Him.

Notice how the same light is in all three places. (Flash the light from one poster to the other.) God is not the link of light that is a bulb in the projector. He is the light that shines through all history and into all eternity. His light shows us the way to live in His love today. His light shows us He will come to take us to live with Him forever.